PLANNING AND DEVELOPMENT

A CASE OF TWO
NOVA SCOTIA COMMUNITIES

A. PAUL PROSS

Institute of Public Affairs
Dalhousie University
Halifax, Canada

FOREWORD

The prime concern of economic development planning, particularly in Nova Scotia, has been provision of jobs in the attack on unemployment, underemployment, and low incomes. Urgent and stubborn problems of attracting new employment-creating enterprises have obscured the equally pressing tasks of planning to meet the needs of people, both present residents and newcomers, in the communities receiving new industry. Paul Pross' study of planning and development at Bridgewater and Port Hawkesbury, Nova Scotia, demonstrates that community and people, responding to the impact of new industry, require priority consideration in policy-making, provincial as well as local, in order that they can be assured of real benefits from development. Quality of life cannot be left to chance.

Dr. Pross' study of these two Nova Scotia communities is a significant contribution to the literature of planning, and likely to be the more useful because of its specific case-style focus. Case histories in the field of business are plentiful and have long been accepted as essential tools of reference and of education by businessmen and students of private sector management. By contrast, similar case studies in public administration are scarce for a number of reasons, including greater complexity and particular sensitivities as well as the problem of sources. Yet the value of case materials is no less important to the public administrator, elected or appointed, and to the concerned citizen.

Dr. Pross holds a joint appointment at Dalhousie University as Research Associate, Institute of Public Affairs, and Associate Professor, School of Public Administration. He is a visiting professor at Carleton University in 1975-76.

A grant of the Canadian Council on Urban and Regional Research supported the necessary research. The Institute of Public Affairs is grateful for this and other assistance from the Council, which has been of vital assistance in the development of the research program of the Institute's Regional and Urban Studies Centre during the past decade.

Guy Henson

Director
Institute of Public Affairs
Dalhousie University

iii

PREFACE

Planning and Development: The Case of Two Nova Scotia Communities is a study of steps taken in Bridgewater and Port Hawkesbury to meet the impact of economic development. The study pays particular attention to the development role of the provincial government and its relations with the two communities. It finds that the provincial government is the most influential actor in the development process and argues that fragmented administrative responsibility and agency independence at the provincial level inhibited efforts at all three levels of government to help both communities make an orderly adjustment to economic development.

The study argues that closer coordination of social and economic development planning is a prerequisite for future industrial expansion in Nova Scotia. It suggest that development policy should be guided by the assumption that the capacity of communities to absorb industrial development will vary with the size of their population and the complexity of their social, political, and economic systems. The larger and more varied a community, the more easily will it adapt to the infusion of new people and new industry; provincial policy, therefore, should support the development of community social infrastructure as well as physical infrastructure.

The conclusions reached in this study are based on interviews with many individuals familiar with the recent history of Port Hawkesbury and Bridgewater. As well, numerous consultants' reports, newspapers, government documents, and the few available academic studies were culled for relevant material.

A major difficulty has been obtaining useful statistical support for the conclusions to which the research has led. Specific information concerning the industrial structure of these communities is not publicly available. Much social data is irretrievably buried in provincial and regional aggregate statistics. Finally, many of the events discussed here occurred too recently to be analysed and reported in the conventional sources.

I am grateful to the many people who have witnessed the recent expansion of Bridgewater and Port Hawkesbury and who gave a great deal of their time to explain their perceptions of the development cycle. In particular, I should like to thank Mr. John Hirtle, Mayor of

Bridgewater; Mr. W.J. MacLean, Mayor of Port Hawkesbury; Mr. Alex Harris, Development Co-ordinator for the Strait; and Mr. Hector Hortie, Regional Director-General for the Department of Regional Economic Expansion.

Michel-Charles Tadros assisted me in carrying out the interviews and in preparing data for the study. His help was much appreciated, as was that of my colleagues at the Institute of Public Affairs, Kell Antoft, Don Clairmont, Jim McNiven, Tom Rath, and Scott Wood - who reviewed an earlier draft - and Olga Neal and Kathleen Wallace, who typed the manuscript. I am also grateful for Margaret Dingley's rigorous editing of the final draft.

Finally, I wish to express my appreciation to the Canadian Council for Urban and Regional Research, whose research grant made this study possible.

A. Paul Pross

CONTENTS

TABLES

FIGURES

I. INTRODUCTION

Nova Scotia's quest for industrial development has aroused a great deal of controversy;[1] so much, in fact, that its most spectacular failure, the Deuterium heavy water plant at Glace Bay, is a national by-word for government ineptitude in high technology development. Lesser disasters have earned the province a reputation as a place to which "forced growth" has attracted numerous unstable companies ready to batten temporarily on low wages and government handouts. Even success has aroused more criticism than congratulation. The location of Michelin Tire Company plants in Granton and Bridgewater earned the opprobrium of organized labour, which objected to the company's "no union" philosophy, and of tire manufacturers in Ontario and the United States, who objected to the Canadian government assisting this powerful multinational firm.

The debate, however, has centred on the economic aspects of development, on the jobs created, the incentives provided, the vetting of promoters and their schemes, and the competitive nature of provincial development policies. Very little interest has been shown in the process of adaptation experienced by the communities that have provided homes and labour forces for the new industries. Specifically, the function of planning for industrial change in Nova Scotia has received minimal attention.

This study attempts to fill that vacuum in part by examining the process of industrial development in two Nova Scotia communities, Port Hawkesbury and Bridgewater.

These communities have been chosen because in their case industrial development has been successful and it has been extensive. Each has had to deal with the problem of absorbing industries employing upwards of 1,000 men and women.[2] Furthermore, although Bridgewater and its region was more populous and affluent than Port Hawkesbury, both communities had fewer than five thousand inhabitants when development began; consequently, development could have been expected to have had a noticeable impact. A further point of similarity stemmed from the fact that neither community could have achieved industrial development without assistance from senior governments. The role of the federal and provincial governments in the development experience would therefore be of interest.

1

The difference between the two communities also made their comparison appealing. Michelin brought as many jobs to Bridgewater as Canadian General Electric, Nova Scotia Forest Industries, Gulf Oil Canada Limited, and others brought to Point Tupper. Yet Bridgewater experienced very little of the disruption we associate with Port Hawkesbury. Again, Port Hawkesbury, as part of a designated area, was of great interest to federal and provincial governments. Both expended considerable effort in attracting industry to nearby Point Tupper and took a part in community planning. Bridgewater, on the other hand, was not part of a special area, and rather than being the object of senior government solicitude, tends to pride itself on its independence. What effect did these cultural and policy-inspired differences have on the two communities' approaches to coping with developing? Finally, Port Hawkesbury lives in the future as much as the present. It could become the centre of a major industrial region. Bridgewater, the centre of a provincial region, does not expect to provide for a population appreciably larger than its present one. Its decision-making parameters are definable, those of Port Hawkesbury are elusive. Surely this contrasting certitude and suspense must affect the process of planning for development?

These points of similarity and of comparison guided the research from its beginning, although as the project developed certain aspects inevitably gained in interest as others receded. Yet the reader will be struck immediately by the very different focus that develops in each of the case studies. In Bridgewater the paramount issues rapidly become the planning process itself and the problem of citizen participation. For Port Hawkesbury similar efforts, significant though they were, became lost in the frenzy of coping with construction booms and providing the basic amenities of a medium sized town.

One feature of the development experience soon came to dominate the findings of the study. That was the role played by the provincial government. Again and again problems in anticipating the demands of expansion were attributed to the Province. Repeatedly, delays in meeting urgent deadlines were blamed on provincial authorities. Frustration with provincial indecision and anger with the lack of provincial leadership surfaced in virtually every interview we conducted with municipal, federal, and sometimes even provincial officials. The role of the province, which we had always assumed was important, became central and largely negative. Necessarily, a chapter had to be devoted to an analysis of provincial development.

A study of this sort is duty bound to go beyond analysis. The problems examined are immediate. The questions they raise are bound to occur in other contexts. In Nova Scotia, for example, provincial officials have raised the possibility that construction of a steel mill will draw to the Cape Breton community of Gabarus a development comparable to those examined here. The study must,

2

then, move out from the cover of armchair dissection and have the temerity to argue for a better way of doing things. The last chapter of this study has tried to do so, basing proposals on the need for reform of the provincial policy process and recognition of both the competence of municipal authorities and the variety of community needs.

II. BRIDGEWATER:
THE ENTREPRENEURIAL APPROACH

Roots: The Power of Positive Thinking

Bridgewater's adjustment to industrial development is generally regarded as a model of its kind. According to the *Graham Report,*

> Bridgewater in 1970 was able to combine (i) local leadership to focus local effort, recognize opportunities, and spearhead action; (ii) a town council that appeared willing and able to lead; (iii) no major unsolved local issues to get in the way of needed action; (iv) access to sound, imaginative technical assistance from a competent and trusted planning consultant who was familiar with the area; and (v) a local spirit of self-reliance, which caused the town to look to its own resources rather than wait for some outside force, such as the provincial government, to take the lead. Put together, this combination provided fertile ground for responsive planning and for public involvement, which contributed to constructive change.[1]

In a similar vein, the Department of Regional Economic Expansion (DREE) has immortalized Bridgewater's experience in a film, "From the Middle of Nowhere", which extols the virtues of combining industrial development, environmental protection, and citizen participation.

It can be expected, then, that in Bridgewater's experience there were techniques of adjustment and approaches to development problems that might well be imitated by other communities. Conversely, Bridgewater's endeavours being the product of human beings and their organizations, it should be found that some of these techniques and approaches need to be improved, or simply forgotten. Finally, since industrial development is an international phenomenon influenced by remote economic and political events, it will undoubtedly be found that Bridgewater's experience has in a number of ways been similar to that of the Strait communities, indicating core problems that require modified approaches on the part of senior as well as municipal governments.

Established in the late eighteenth century as an outpost of Lunenburg, Bridgewater is now the commercial and industrial centre of Lunenburg County. Its progression is attributable to its location and to a tradition of entrepreneurship. Since the middle of the nineteenth century, the LaHave River has brought shipping inland to the town's wharves. For many years timber and produce were carried downstream from Bridgewater's sawmills and markets. As water transportation gave way to overland communication links within the province, the LaHave again determined the town's continued growth, this time because Bridgewater was a place at which the river could be crossed.

The first bridge was built by the 1830s; so were the first school and post office. About that time a road linked the settlement with Lunenburg and, therefore, Halifax. The 1860s saw the first real "economic take-off" with the establishment at Bridgewater of the chief operations of the Davison Lumber Company, one of the province's largest lumber operations. Originally located on the unnavigable Medway River, the company moved to Bridgewater because of its situation at tidehead. The company at this time operated on 200,000 acres along the LaHave, Medway, and Nictau Rivers and in 1904, a year after its sale to American interests, reported a supply area of a million acres in the province - second only to the combined acreage of Halifax firms - and an output of 23,000,000 superficial feet, which was comparable to the annual production of major operators in Ontario's Georgian Bay area, then considered to be among the continent's leaders.[2]

The company, by its very existence, encouraged the growth of transportation facilities. It operated a railway into the centre of the province, along the LaHave River, and its founder played a large part in ensuring that the town served as a terminal for the railway connecting the coastal communities of the south shore. From the 1890s Bridgewater became the centre of various transportation links and, as a result, important as a trading centre. Connected by railroad with Halifax, the town flourished. It had a major lumbering industry, an iron foundry, a tannery, a carding mill, a grist mill, and even enjoyed a brief gold rush when gold was discovered nearby.

Local government arrived in 1873, when the town was recognized as a district. In 1899 incorporation was achieved, and in the same year a fire destroyed most of the commercial centre. Despite the setback, the town prospered and, by the 1920s, Bridgewater was an important economic centre for the south shore. *Canada East* magazine of March 1931 described its booming economy in an article entitled "Bridgewater: The Hub of the South Shore". As an industrial centre, the town had the largest woodworking plant in the Maritimes, doing business all over Nova Scotia; it had the largest marine engine plant in Canada, with branches in every East Coast port and in St. John's, Newfoundland. Bridgewater was a communications centre, with excellent rail communication with Halifax; and, finally, it was a market centre for the surrounding rich farming and fruit-growing areas of the south shore. The town was really "a thriving little city".

The depression saw Bridgewater go through the familiar cycle of events. The lumbering industry, the staple of its growth during the nineteenth century and the early part of the twentieth century, had declined considerably. At the same time, fishing became virtually moribund, while trading was confined to minor traffic along the LaHave River and the export of a few lumber products. The thirties were as depressed in Bridgewater as elsewhere. One industry that did keep going was the Acadia Gas Engine Company. Another company, Telfer-Crowe Woodworkers, which has since become H.W. Brady, also kept going. This provided a base for activity during the war, at which time Acadia in particular operated at full capacity. Following the war, Acadia continued to operate until the preferential tariff on small marine engines was removed. American companies soon dominated its traditional markets and Acadia, which had not kept up to date on its manufacturing methods, had to be sold to a large British concern.

The decline of Acadia Gas Engine Company, however, came at roughly the same time as the increasing preeminence of the town as a commercial centre. Towards the end of the 1950s, a number of chain stores began establishing operations in the town. In the 1960s this led to the building of a shopping centre which recently has been joined by two others.

At present Bridgewater has a population of more than 5,231 (1971), growing at a rate of 12 per cent between 1951 and 1961 and 16 per cent between 1961 and 1971, a consistently faster rate than that of other communities in the region.[3] Twenty-five per cent of workers engaged in manufacturing employment in Lunenburg County were located in Bridgewater in 1971, compared to 12 per cent in 1968. Retail sales in 1966 mounted to $15,673,000 ($3,296 per capita) or 30.8 per cent of retail sales in the Queens-Lunenburg region, so that:

> In the hierarchy of retail and wholesale trade and community business and personal services, Bridgewater now stands as the undisputed centre of the county. In recent years this advantage over other centres has been extended, particularly in the retail sector with expansion of several facilities. As well as being the base of the greatest population concentration in the county, it is geographically situated at the crossroads of the main highway # 3 and the routes which follow up and down both sides of the LaHave River. Its area of trade for comparison goods extends to Mill Village in Queens County on the west, to Western Shore on the east, and Springfield on the north. This area comprises a population of over 30,000.[4]

Value of building permits issued between 1968 and 1974 totalled over $13.7 million, with the major portions representing construction of the Michelin Tire Plant and two new shopping centres. Other facilities, such as motels, have also been constructed. With the location of county municipal offices near the town limits, the construction in the town of a regional vocational school enrolling 400 students, and the maintenance of an 86-bed hospital and various government regional offices at Bridgewater, the town can claim to be the governmental service centre for the south shore. Location of CKBW-Bridgewater also makes it the only town between Halifax and Yarmouth possessing a radio station.

Bridgewater's capacity to take advantage of the potential of the town's site owes a good deal to a tradition of enterprise among its leading figures, a tradition that continues today and is closely related to what the *Graham Report* described as "a local spirit of self-reliance".

As Roy George has pointed out, this is a tradition that is too often missing from the Nova Scotia scene, with unhappy consequences for the province:

> The lack of an adequate supply of entrepreneurship was a serious matter for Nova Scotia, since the role of the entrepreneur is so crucial to any organization. If new business opportunities are not ferreted out and exploited energetically, the progress of the region is bound to be retarded.[5]

Enterprise is a tradition that dates from Bridgewater's earliest days:

> When James Starratt, 'a pushing enterprising man', rode from Annapolis County in 1828, the site of the present town was nearly all forest to the river's brink. Nonetheless he built a hotel on a wharf beside the recently finished bridge over the LaHave.[6]

Eighteen years later the hustle and bustle that typified Starratt and his neighbours earned the disapproval of the Rev. E.E.B. Nichols. At Bridgewater, he wrote, "a cluster of some thirty dwellings form the village - there are members of nine different denominations among them - and the only thing in which they agree is to make as much money as they can in any way that they can."[7]

In the nineteenth century Bridgewater's spirit of enterprise was epitomized by the aggressiveness of E.D. Davison* who, in the process of extending one of Nova Scotia's largest lumbering operations, contributed a great deal to Bridgewater's development as a port and secured for the town an important position in the railway system that tied together the province's south shore during the second

---

*Davison claimed, for example, to be the first operator in the province to use a steam driven sawmill. His energies were expended on civic affairs as well as business concerns. He was Mayor of Bridgewater and MLA (Defebaugh, *op.cit.*, p. 249).

half of the nineteenth century. Today it is expressed in the town's vigorous commercial activities and its pursuit of industrial development. Much of this activity has taken place at the local government level.

Nova Scotians in the early 1960s were preoccupied with the efforts of Robert Stanfield to persuade them to "stop bewailing their handicaps and . . . start bestirring themselves".[8] Establishing provincial structures, such as Industrial Estates Limited (IEL) and Voluntary Economic Planning, to promote and plan for economic development, and working with the Diefenbaker government to create parallel regional bodies such as the Atlantic Development Board, the Stanfield government "convinced [the people of Nova scotia] that they did not have to remain a backwater, retarded and depressed. He convinced them that they had a future worth working for."[9]

Bridgewater shared in the renaissance. Through its Board of Trade, leaders of the business community began an organized effort to attract new industry to the town. In 1965, a Board of Trade delegation attending a community planning conference sponsored by the Nova Scotia Division, Community Planning Association of Canada, and the Institute of Public Affairs, Dalhousie University, was impressed by a report on the success of the Truro Industrial Development Commission in attracting industry to that community. One of the members of the delegation was John F. Hirtle, now the Mayor of Bridgewater and, for many years, a leading figure in promoting the town's development. On returning from the planning conference, he and his colleagues lost no time in recommending that the town take advantage of recently enacted provincial legislation and establish an Industrial Development Commission of its own.

Under the provisions of the provincial legislation the Bridgewater Industrial Commission, a municipally appointed commission, was empowered to "solicit and encourage the establishment and development of new industry. . .to encourage the expansion of existing industry. . .[and] to recommend zoning by-laws, provision of industrial sites, measures concerning the effects of taxation" and so on.[10] In Hirtle's view, however, the Commission's most significant feature lay in its authority to buy land in the name of the town for industrial development. Its creation translated the development thrust of the Board of Trade to the local government level. It provided the local authorities with an organizational arm capable of focusing on development. It provided that arm with local expertise through the co-optation process. It gave the business community a point of access to local government expressly concerned with the development issue. It extended to the Commission the authority necessary to ensure that the town could meet the locational needs of new industry and provided a mechanism for communication, not only with industry but with the provincial development authorities.

9

The Commission gave new impetus to the development cause. Contact was made with the Atlantic Development Board, which acknowledged Bridgewater's potential, and with provincial agencies. At the urging of the Commission the town council engaged a consulting firm to assess local development possibilities. The consultant recommended the establishment of a 25-acre industrial park. At the same time, the IDC determined on an industrial strategy that treated development as important, but resolved "not to destroy the town".[11] Bridgewater's quiet, small-town atmosphere was an asset worth preserving, and to retain it the town had to exert a reasonable control over its own enviroment. Planning was therefore essential.

The Industrial Development Commission was initiated in 1965 and, though it achieved no major public breakthrough in the next few years, did contribute to the community's perception of itself as "go ahead". This perception was further bolstered by expansion of commercial activity in the town. By 1966, Bridgewater, with 9.7 per cent of the Queens-Lunenburg population, was handling 30.8 per cent of the region's retail sales. Although figures for subsequent years are not available, the construction of the first shopping centre and expansion of parking facilities in the downtown area are felt, in the region, to have accelerated the town's domination of commercial activity in Queens and Lunenburg Counties. Construction of a regional vocational school, which was opened in 1969, served to enhance the region's capacity to develop trained personnel, and the relocation of the Municipality of Lunenburg's offices from the town of Lunenburg to the outskirts of Bridgewater formally recognized the town's preeminence in Lunenburg County.

Major development, however, eluded Bridgewater until the fall of 1968, when town officials noted in the provincial press that the Michelin Tire Company, a major French tire manufacturer, was considering Nova Scotia as the location for a North American operation. John Hirtle, who with Walter Logan was then co-chairman of the Industrial Development Commission, sought information from IEL's president, Robert Manuge, but was told that Manuge "didn't know anything about it."[12] In actuality, Manuge had been in contact with the Michelin firm since November 1967 [13] and had included Bridgewater in a tour of Nova Scotia communities arranged early in 1968 for Daniel LeJaune, Michelin's vice-president of plant expansion. Michelin had not been impressed with the town. Happily unaware of this, Hirtle and Logan now took steps that have since passed into the town's store of legends and have done much to enhance Bridgewater's claim to enterprise and self-reliance.

Not content with Manuge's reticence, Hirtle and Logan learnt more about the Michelin company from the local Michelin dealer, Mel Pickings. Noting its paternalistic personnel policies, as well as its highly desirable stability, they composed a letter to the company that stressed the town's social amenities in addition to its abundant supplies of water for industrial purposes and its proposed industrial park. As a final touch, the letter was translated into French by Logan's daughter, a local teacher. Provincial officials have since claimed that the letter had little effect on the Michelin decision, but have not been able to deny Michelin officials' own assertion that it prompted head office to direct LeJaune to take another look at Bridgewater. This he did on May 11, 1969. He noted the town's cleanliness and neatness and the diligence with which people looked after their properties, and reported favourably to his colleagues. Construction of the Bridgewater plant began in 1970.

Planning for Social Development

Municipal leaders and the Industrial Development Commission were quick to appreciate the social implications of attracting to Bridgewater an industry that would employ initially a labour force of 500 and eventually more than 1,000. A concern for planned social as well as economic development manifested itself and was soon given concrete expression.

Not long after John Hirtle gained office as Mayor, in 1970, the town entered into discussions with the Department of Municipal Affairs, Community Planning Division.* On the Division's advice, a local Planning Advisory Committee was appointed. On the 22nd of March, 1971, the Department of Municipal Affairs and the Planning Advisory Committee discussed a report prepared for the Committee by the Community Planning Division. The report, entitled "Planning for Development in the Bridgewater Area", recommended working out a short-term development strategy for the town and surrounding area by identifying expected development, pinpointing the actions needed to meet the consequent demands, and setting up processes for taking those actions. The major problem was seen as an urgent need for residential expansion. The Planning Advisory Committee agreed to undertake initial planning activity and, with the assistance of the provincial planning staff and the Nova Scotia Housing Commission, developed a Housing Work Group. Further discussions took place in

*Under the Nova Scotia Planning Act (*Statutes of Nova Scotia, 1969,* c. 16), it is provided that the Minister of Municipal Affairs, operating through the Department's Community Planning Division, is responsible for formally initiating planning activity, providing the necessary technical support, giving final approval for plans and by-laws and, in special cases, intervening directly in municipal planning administration. The Province also has a considerable financial interest in local planning.

Section 22 of the Planning Act provides that a council may appoint a planning advisory committee composed of council members and others, with the majority drawn from council. The committee may not usurp council's final authority in adopting a municipal plan. Adoption can only be achieved through a by-law passed by a majority vote of the whole council (s. 14), and approved by the Minister of Municipal Affairs.

June of 1971, when the Planning Division presented the Planning Advisory Committee with a "short-term planning program". This set out the key issues, backed up with detailed information outlining the projected short-term impact of the Michelin plant on the town, and identified two main alternative development patterns. It recommended that the town, with provincial assistance, commission a planning study in two parts, the first to meet the short-term development needs, including identifying the best pattern for development, and the second developing a longer-term plan. A report on the meeting was accompanied by a proposal by Harold Verge, a planner familiar with the Bridgewater area, to carry out the first part of the plan. This proposal was subsequently accepted by the town.

Harold Verge has a reputation in Nova Scotia for innovative planning. A native of Bridgewater, his work in promoting community involvement in Pictou County's development has been widely recognized. His proposed Bridgewater "planning blitz" seemed equally promising as a first step towards a continuing community-wide participation in establishing guidelines for the town's growth.

The "planning blitz" was to be a short-cut to establishing the town's major objectives and planning needs, but it nevertheless embodied the essential features of Verge's approach to planning. This entails exciting general public interest in the planning process and then ensuring that the desire to participate is sustained by a readily available pool of technical expertise and the development of organizational capacity. The former is usually drawn from government agencies; the latter is created through the work of Verge and his colleagues, who see themselves as the midwives of local planning capability rather than technical planning consultants charged with drawing up a specific design with accompanying by-laws.

The Bridgewater situation appeared to offer an ideal occasion for the application of Verge's technique. It possessed an enterprising group of businessmen already involved in the planning process; a well-defined planning objective; and local leadership convinced that a sound town plan had to be developed. It remained only to expand the base of citizen participation in the planning process and to bring technical knowledge to bear on the problems involved.

The blitz took place in July 1971:

> With financial assistance from the Municipal Affairs Department, Verge pulled together all the provincial and federal expertise around and, within two weeks, had a pretty good assessment of the town's opportunities for investment.[14]

The blitz sessions, which were carried out at the Vocational School, were open to the public and, as a result of intensive preliminary publicity, attracted more than 300 participants. The planning team itself included staff drawn from the Community Planning Division, the Provincial Cabinet Office, the Nova Scotia Department of Development, the federal and regional offices of DREE, as well as members of the Town Council, the Planning Advisory Committee, Industrial Development Commission, and Parks Commission, local consulting engineers and other local people with technical knowledge, and, of course, the planner's own staff. The sessions were also attended by other personnel from government departments who were free to observe or comment on the issues as they were discussed and plans as they were developed. The blitz thus achieved the objective of putting the local community in touch with technical people and added an unusual bonus. By bringing so many specialists together on the site itself, Verge encouraged an exchange of ideas and information between the experts themselves and the general public, and this innovation gave greater depth to both local and professional understanding of the challenges facing the town.

Public Participation: High Hopes and Retrenchment
The exercise also achieved Verge's objective of creating a broad-based community planning group. The Community Planning Council, which emerged from the blitz, represented a cross-section of the community. A Department of Agriculture community development worker, Alan Connor, was appointed to organize the Planning Council, which was "to provide a communications vehicle for the citizens and their elected representatives",[15] to be effected through development of close working relations between the CPC, the Town Council and the Planning Advisory Committee. Verge reasoned:

> In this way there are no surprises . . . When land use changes are requested . . . the whole question is aired fully and the Town Council knows what its citizens are thinking . . . . This also applies to other areas as well.
>
> Confrontation, or the formation of pressure groups, should not be necessary . . . . It is important to develop good rapport and have everything out in the open.[16]

The Community Planning Council was warmly endorsed by the Town Council, and its first organizational meeting attracted fifty representatives of community organizations, as well as a cross-section of individuals from Bridgewater society.[17] During the subsequent winter, a series of meetings discussed various aspects of community planning. At these, "committees are appointed . . . and it is the responsibility of each committee to expand so that people from all walks of life in Bridgewater will have a voice in community development. These committees, of which there may be a dozen or

Figure 1

MAJOR SITES REFERRED TO IN TEXT:

TOWN OF BRIDGEWATER

1. South Shore Mall (1974)
2. Miller Property
3. Bridgewater Mall (1975)
4. Approximate location of Highway 103 bypass and interchange
5. Industrial estate and Michelin plant
6. Vocational School
7. Bridgewater Shopping Centre (1960s)
8. South Shore Exhibition
9. Golf Course
10. Park, swimming pool and Desbrisay museum

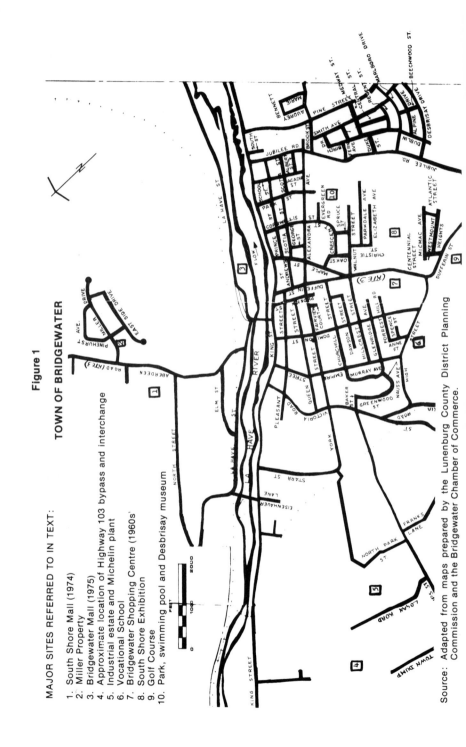

Source: Adapted from maps prepared by the Lunenburg County District Planning Commission and the Bridgewater Chamber of Commerce.

14

more, will elect or appoint representatives to form the main Citizens' Planning Group, which will communicate with and advise the Town Council on its planning authority."[18]

This period, from July 1971 to mid-1972, marked the high point of planning activity and interest in citizen participation in Bridgewater. Anticipating development, not yet deeply involved in the actuality, the community exhibited a good deal of interest in planning for the future and local officials demonstrated a concern for ensuring that the average citizen have as much opportunity as possible to participate in the planning process. Verge himself saw the blitz as a success. He estimated that it made available to the town considerable planning expertise at minimal cost and that it had brought members of the community into active participation in the planning process. This process, furthermore, focused "less on projected trends than on setting a vision of what the community could be, establishing a planning process which begins realizing that vision while building community confidence and reliance."[19]

Verge presented a planning study to Town Council early in August 1971. This summarized the results of the planning blitz and identified five major influences that constituted, in Verge's view, the foundations upon which a development plan could be built. These influences were:

1. the existence of the Industrial Commission which, together with the Town Council, constituted a potentially workable development mechanism;
2. a new, large industry, ready to open its doors to a work force projected to reach 650 to 700 persons;
3. the prospect of Highway 103, which was plotted by the Nova Scotia Department of Highways to pass over 206 acres of town-owned land (a part being the 126-acre industrial park) and scheduled for completion in 1975;
4. the first stages of an extensive pollution abatement program, well under way, including a sewage treatment plant which would meet the requirements of a population of 9,000;
5. a general feeling of optimism on the part of town residents that Bridgewater's future was more promising than it had been for years.[20]

Verge's study formed the basis for subsequent planning activities.

By November 1971, the Town Council adopted "resolutions establishing policy and programs of the Town of Bridgewater respecting planning", a short-term development plan that established a planning process, setting out the town's development objectives and policy, arranging for needed technical capabilities, setting up the Development Commission as the town's Developmental and Housing Agency, firmly establishing the principle of community involvement, and taking steps to set up the Community Planning Council. That body met for the first time in December 1971; with assistance from Alan Connor of the Department of Agriculture and Marketing and Dr. Grace Maynard of DREE, organized a Steering Committee; and, over the winter, set up working groups to study and report upon topics of special interest.

The Bridgewater Industrial Development Commission was also active. Alert to the need for social planning to run parallel to industrial development planning, the Commission, in the fall of 1971, had embraced its social role to such an extent that it changed its name from Industrial Development Commission to the Bridgewater Development Commission. Chaired by Mr. Sally Nafthal, the Commission undertook ·a variety of socially oriented activities, including the purchase of the Miller property, a major property of 400 acres on the east side of the LaHave River, most of it within the town boundaries, which was proposed in the planning study for residential expansion. The Commission also negotiated with the Department of Highways to create a commercial service area on either side of the new highway by-pass and the industrial park area, a negotiation which proved to be protracted and the cause of considerable local dissension. As well, the Commission successfully petitioned the Province to finance a feasibility study of recreational and commercial development in the Bridgewater area. Other Commission activities included the attempt to rationalize land use in the town through negotiation with the South Shore Exposition, which utilized its grounds within the town area for less than one week a year, and with the Golf Course, which is considering relocation near the Miller property.

At this point Bridgewater entered the most critical phase of the planning process, the taking of hard decisions and the closing off of options to individuals and groups in the community that might otherwise have benefited from development activities. In Bridgewater, as elsewhere, initial enthusiasm gave way to disagreement, friction, and a degree of disillusionment in the community. Discontent focused on two phases of the planning exercise. First, leading members of the community were not prepared for the complex adjustment of roles that occurs in the process of developing citizen participation. Nor were they skilled in the business of achieving accommodation between citizenry and government through public discussion. Second, the town found the implementation of a novel planning procedure somewhat more difficult than it had anticipated. Particularly, it encountered difficulties in its relations with the provincial government.

Prior to the blitz, the business community had been the chief participant in the planning process. It had been the part of the community most deeply involved in bringing the Michelin plant to Bridgewater. Its chief instrument of participation, developed in conjunction with government, was the Bridgewater Industrial

Development Commission. As we have noted, the Michelin decision led to the recognition that development would take place at the social as well as the economic level and, consequently, that an organizational thrust similar to that which had focused on industrial development would have to provide for the new social needs. Thus, the Bridgewater Industrial Development Commission became the Bridgewater Development Commission and turned its attention to land assembly projects and promoting measures that would be socially beneficial as well as economically rewarding. There is no doubt that the Commission achieved several important goals, goals that were significant from a planning point of view and from the point of view of social benefit; however, though it broadened its activities, the Commission did not expand its base beyound the business community. In consequence it encountered opposition from two directions.

First, a number of business leaders objected to the local government, through the Commission, becoming involved in land assembly and development. They argued that this activity was best carried out by the private sector. In other words, although the Commission continued to secure the support of senior local officials, it lost its legitimacy in the eyes of some of its supporters. Furthermore, these disaffected supporters sought to stifle the social policy initiatives of the Commission and Council by appealing directly to provincial officials, thus, in the view of the Mayor, weakening both the Commission and the negotiating position of the Council.

The second consequence of the Commission's failure to achieve a membership base commensurate with its expanded mission emerged during the planning blitz. The open forum of the blitz provided an opportunity for new elements in the community to articulate their interests and to coalesce. It attracted individuals who represented the non-business sector of the community, came from the less affluent parts of town, were concerned about events in those parts of town, and had not previously enjoyed organized access to Bridgewater's decision making processes. The Community Planning Council became their instrument. Even though it had been visualized as a necessary consequence of the planning blitz and also attracted individuals who had played a part in the work of the Industrial Development Commission, inevitably as time passed the Development Commission and the Community Planning Council came to represent the institutionalization of Bridgewater's traditional cleavages between the dominant business community and those who felt that they had no place in the community power structure.

Town Council fostered this pattern by its treatment of the Community Planning Council. It recognized the CPC and committed itself to providing financial as well as moral support to the organization, but the CPC was not given the same status as the

Development Commission; that is, it was not recognized as a semi-official branch of local government. Hence, while "business leaders in the community were [permitted] to officially be part of public decision making",[21] the Planning Council was not official. Its reports "received careful consideration and are reflected in many policies concerning the Development Plan".[22]

The practical difficulties of planning for development soon created an issue that emphasized the social and economic cleavages we have just described and cast in doubt the future of citizen participation in Bridgewater. The point of dispute was the location of a highway by-pass and major interchange. The dispute occurred in the fall of 1972 and involved two pieces of property in the northern part of town, between St. Phillips Street and King Street, which had been owned by the town for several years. The first, the town dump, had been purchased in 1954 and the second, the industrial park, in 1966. By the fall of 1972, the park had a major tenant, Michelin, and it appeared eminently sensible to provincial and local planners that the dump site should be the site of the Bridgewater section of Highway 103, a limited access highway linking Halifax and Yarmouth, and that it should also be the site of an interchange that would serve both the western bank of the LaHave River and the industrial park. Unfortunately, while this arrangement promised to expand the area and enhance the merits of the industrial park, and so improve the town's tax base, it also meant the demolition of some dozen houses owned or occupied by lower income families. Their feelings were expressed by Kathleen Pentz, a prominent member of the Community Planning Council:

> Bridgewater is a town divided. It is divided geographically by the LaHave River, and it is divided economically.
> Lower income earners tend to live in the outlying areas, especially in the region of St. Phillips and King Streets, north of the town centre. This area has grown topsyturvy, the houses in many cases having been built by the owners. Some do not have adequate sewer and water services and there are very few sidewalks. With the exception of a small park on St. Phillips Street, recently installed for a total cost of $500, there is nothing in the way of recreational facilities. The residents of that same street have been asking for a traffic light for years - to no avail. The area has no representation on the town council.
> In contrast, the central section of Bridgewater, on the western side of the river, has more expensive housing, adequate sewer and water services, two commercial areas, three schools, and numerous recreational facilities, some of which have cost the residents of Bridgewater an enormous amount of money. Because the more influential citizens live in the area, their needs are taken into account more readily than the needs of those who have the misfortune to live either in the north or on the east side of the LaHave River.[23]

The North King Street residents felt that the interchange decision epitomized their lack of influence with Town Council. They had not been consulted during consideration of the route for the new highway

18

and their concerns had not been taken into account. A residents' association was formed, which proposed that the highway be located half a mile north in vacant land owned by the Scott Paper Company. The group met with the Community Planning Council and with provincial and town officials and presented a petition bearing some 1,500 names to Town Council. These meetings were generally unsuccessful. The CPC officially steered clear of the dispute, although individual members supported the King Street residents, and Town Council, while quarrelling with the provincial Highways Department over certain aspects of by-pass and interchange plans, did not support the residents' counter-proposal. The proposal was rejected. Furthermore, the town's decision to extend water services into the area - which, in turn, threatened to involve further demolitions - added to the discontent of the King Street residents, but their objections were largely ineffectual.

The North King Street issue influenced the development of citizen participation in Bridgewater in three ways. First, it led to disillusionment on the part of residents in the King Street area and, to a lesser extent, elsewhere in the town with the participatory process. They concluded that Town Council was not sincerely supporting citizen participation. The "high-handed" manner in which the location decision had been taken seemed ample proof of that:

It was not until the King Street residents had become irate enough to form an organization and protest to the Town Council, that the official planning bodies tried to explain the situation. They did not effectively accomplish this. To the delegation, it was one more instance of those in the centre of town benefitting over those in the north. The council had asked them to think of the benefit and development of Bridgewater as a whole, but the residents wondered when Bridgewater had ever considered the benefits of those living on North King.24

Secondly, the dispute led to the collapse of the Community Planning Council, the chief vehicle for citizen participation in Bridgewater. The CPC's decision to steer clear of the King Street issue had followed intense internal dispute. Although the proponents of neutrality had ensured the CPC's non-involvement, the personal antagonism that developed during the dispute - particularly over the publicity given the issues by supporters of the residents - undermined the viability of the organization. The executive could no longer work together; membership dropped; and the CPC collapsed.

The third effect of the issue was to focus attention at the Town Council level on the role that citizens' groups could be allowed to play in the decision making process. Relations between the groups and the Town Council were strained, even though both sides felt that citizen participation and the effort being made were important and beneficial to development in the town. The Planning Council had encouraged the citizens to develop very high expectations of their involvement, and to expect their advice to be taken completely by Town Council. The North King Street group felt "that the Council, to which they had gone seeking support, was not really willing to give that support."[25] The Town Council, on the other hand, saw itself as the final arbiter in disputes within the community and felt that it was justified in seeing presentations from Planning Council and other groups as merely parts of a series of inputs. The North King Street issue, consequently, served as the occasion for the Town Council to assert its preeminent role in local decision making. It did not, unfortunately, appear to lead to more intensive consideration of the role of citizen participation in the early stages of community decision making.

Although the CPC disappeared, the drive to full citizen participation did not. Shortly thereafter a new group, the Citizens' Advisory Committee, was formed and a newcomer to Bridgewater, Lloyd Campbell, was persuaded to act as chairman. A series of meetings were held with individuals like Harold Verge in an attempt to excite more interest, and Campbell himself followed a policy of co-opting into the organization people who were opinion leaders within significant segments of the community. Thus, Ella Spence and Robert Manthorne had demonstrated an interest in town affairs by running for elections;[26] both became valuable members of the CAC. Ella Spence represented a particular elite group in the community and had that group's approval, while Robert Manthorne was a leader of the North King Street group. This ensured that the CAC had both a degree of approval from the important groups in the town and people on the executive who were prepared to spend a good deal of time working for the committee. As it turned out, the group, although much smaller than originally intended during the planning blitz, proved remarkably dedicated to consideration of the community development plan during 1972 and 1973. Its relations with Town Council were reasonably successful and, while the community in general is relatively apathetic - most CAC meetings fail to attract more than twenty to forty members - there has been a sufficient sense of movement in the community and a sufficiently challenging opportunity in the activity of developing a town plan to engage the interest of at least a core group. At any rate, although there have been no major issues for the CAC to deal with, there have been considerable activities for it to undertake in relation to the development and approval of the development plan and the accompanying by-law.

Intergovernmental Relations
As many tensions developed between the town and senior levels of government over the development of the plan as between the town and the citizens' groups. As has been noted, Harold Verge saw in the Bridgewater experience an opportunity to introduce some innovative

planning techniques. The first and most spectacular of these was the planning blitz, an exercise that is still regarded as having been highly successful in the community, one that has heightened interest and enthusiasm for the planning process, and which provided Bridgewater with acces to a great deal of expertise and data within a restricted time frame. Verge's elaborate structure of sector committees, however, failed to develop because of the collapse of the CPC. This denied an important element of organizational support for the central feature of the new scheme, the process of evolving to a position "where there is no separation of the planning and implementation functions."[27]

The consequences of this organizational failure became evident when the plan was forwarded to the Community Planning Division of the Department of Municipal Affairs, which was ultimately responsible for reviewing the town's plan and for recommending the approval of the necessary by-laws. The plan was rejected on the grounds that the planner had not sufficiently consulted the Division, had not provided the conditions under which the Division could monitor the planning process, had not developed by-laws that were technically sound, and had failed to follow accepted practice in the development of population projections. In the view of the Division, the plan as presented was not rigorous enough to be valid as a development plan. Ironically, another basic objection was the emphasis put by Mr. Verge on public participation in the decision making process and the planning of the community. It was felt by the Division that too much public participation was involved and, conversely, not enough technical input. As a result, the plan seemed to the Division more a statement of good intention than a workable document.[28] Had Verge's scheme been fully implemented, it is likely that contact between the Division and the sector committees would have been frequent enough to satisfy the technical planners.

The rejection of the plan created a good deal of hostility in the community towards the provincial government, particularly the Community Planning Division. The mayor objected to its being returned "all shot to hell" and felt that it had fallen victim to professional preconceptions in the Community Planning Division. Others in the community felt that the plan had also been victim of professional wrangling within the Department. It is more likely, however, that Bridgewater's plan failed because the Division was at this time experiencing severe shortages of professional staff, rapid turnover of staff, and a leadership overwhelmed by the multitude and variety of demands placed upon the Division.[29] Faced with problems of this sort, the Division lacked the capacity to maintain continuous liaison with other parts of the Department, let alone individual municipalities, and consequently processed proposed plans, like Bridgewater's, in a disjointed and often arbitrary fashion. Despite local resentment, however, the town proceeded to revise its plan and to submit a more orthodox document. The negotiations between the town and the Community Planning Division are still continuing, amidst a good deal of concern in the community over the length of time involved in the process.[30]

It is extremely unfortunate that the Community Planning Division took so restrictive a view of the development plan. To members of the community, it represented a return to a traditional relationship between the province and the town in which provincial disposal of town proposals are not only handled in an arbitrary and non-consultative fashion, but are delayed an unconscionable period of time. The episode discouraged many who had been interested in the planning process and, of course, led to delay in the town's development activities.

The Department of Municipal Affairs, however, was not the only provincial agency with which the town experienced difficulties. Representatives of both Bridgewater and the Municipality of the District of Lunenburg have expressed disappointment that the provincial Department of Education has not been more helpful in anticipating the rise in school enrolment caused by the influx of Michelin workers.[31] A great deal of difficulty was encountered with the Department of Highways, which proposed the routing of a new trunk highway, Number 103, through the northern part of the town, as has already been noted. Town officials, anxious to locate an interchange on the west side of the LaHave River near to the industrial park, found highway officials difficult to convince and reluctant to accept the town's proposal for an interchange structure which occupied less than the usual space. At the moment this negotiation is still proceeding, as is a negotiation relating to the construction of a second bridge over the LaHave River. In both situations, delay at the departmental level and apparent unwillingness to consider the town's position have led to some bitterness.

Perhaps the most successful feature of Bridgewater's planning activity has been the encouragement it has given to planning throughout Lunenburg County. Although regional and municipal planning has long been a goal of the provincial Community Planning Division, and is required under the Planning Act, progress throughout much of the province has been relatively slow. At the time that Bridgewater became involved in negotiations leading to the establishment of the Michelin plant, however, the state of planning in the province was receiving a considerable push forward from the passage of a new Planning Act and from the decision of the Community Planning Division to decentralize to a degree by locating consultant planners in a number of communities. Bridgewater's advances in the development field alerted its own officials to the need for consultation with the Municipality of Lunenburg, both municipal governments being to some degree affected by large-scale development in Bridgewater. Accordingly, a series of meetings took place in Lunenburg County which led eventually to the creation of the Lunenburg County District Planning Commission, which was formally established in July 1973. The Commission is headed by the Mayor of Bridgewater, Mr. John Hirtle, and is composed of representatives of the Councils of the Municipalities of Chester and the District of Lunenburg, and the Towns of Lunenburg, Mahone Bay, and Bridgewater. It has engaged professional planners and is now involved in the development of a regional plan.

Assessment

Bridgewater's planning has achieved limited success. It has not brought about the extensive community involvement promised during the 1971 planning blitz; a traditional pattern of business-dominated decision making seems to have persisted. Nor does it seem to have led to a consensus within the town about the most desirable pattern of development. The attempt to provide the town with an unusual degree of access to technical expertise also seems to have been generally unsuccessful. The development of a town plan has taken a considerable time, at a period when the pressure of development requires a general understanding of community objectives and alternatives and firm guidelines for investment decisions. Because of the delay in implementing the plan, the plan itself appears to have been influenced by the pattern of development rather than the reverse. Furthermore, while the planning process has achieved a considerable extension of planning activity throughout Lunenburg County, it does not seem to have achieved a parallel improvement in provincial decision making relating to the area. Provincial agencies continue to act unilaterally, slowly, and frequently without much appreciation of local conditions. Finally, despite the town's claim to be avoiding, through planning, the urban blight evident in many centres,[32] a visitor from one of those centres would find many a familiar scene in Bridgewater, particularly in the town's failure to treat the LaHave River as a scenic amenity and its decision to fill in a part of the river to serve as a site for a shopping plaza.

This was, however, Bridgewater's first brush with development planning, and its successes, though limited, were in some cases important. Full-fledged citizen participation fell by the wayside, but a citizens' organization has survived and the possibility of more extensive public involvement has been suggested to the public. A more dynamic community decision making process may eventually result. Similarly, although very tattered, the idea of planning for development has been introduced to the community and has persisted. Through the establishment of a district planning office, a degree of planning expertise has been brought to the area and a base provided for the gradual introduction of planning concepts to the

Lunenburg County region. Finally, while this phase of development activity does not seem to have been much affected by Bridgewater's planning effort, the process itself undoubtedly sharpened local perceptions of the alternatives and opportunities before the town and probably contributed to a fuller understanding of locational decisions made by local businessmen.

Of the various lessons that can be learned from the Bridgewater experience, perhaps the most important relate to the fact that despite its difficulties with the Community Planning Division the town enjoyed a good deal of freedom in developing its own approach to expansion. To a large extent it did not experience the paternalistic and overbearing approach to local government often exhibited by provincial officials in Nova Scotia.

This is in sharp contrast to Port Hawkesbury's experience. The reasons for this contrast will be considered later in this chapter. Attention is drawn to it here in order to underline the importance that a community should attach to appreciating the role it can play in planning for its own development. That role is circumscribed, not only by the specific authority allocated by statute to the community but by the independent mandates of provincial and federal agencies responsible for encouraging development. By appreciating the limited nature of its role, the individual community can take advantage of that aspect of development which it is capable of influencing. It can, for example, familiarize itself with the activities of relevant agencies of senior governments and, where possible, utilize local institutions, such as the Bridgewater Development Commission, to effect close ties with the more important agencies at the senior level. Such ties will, in the long run, assist the community in anticipating development needs and provide an opportunity to promote the town's particular advantages.

Bridgewater's experience also demonstrates (a) the importance of creating a balance between the various sources of input to local government decisions related to development, and (b) the perils of extending an instrument of local government action beyond its legitimate mandate. In the case of Bridgewater, while the Industrial Development Commission performed a valid and useful function in the industrial development field itself, the extension of its mandate without commensurate broadening of its base of support reduced its legitimacy in the business community and contributed to a build-up of tension within the community at large. Instead of working with the Community Planning Council, the Commission became a rival. The CPC's role was not fully worked out from the beginning, and it seems to have laboured throughout its life under the stigma of not being as important as the Development Commission, a situation which exacerbated the feeling of some portions of the community that they were not considered by the Town Council.

Finally, in Bridgewater is seen yet another instance of the difficulties inherent in that vital adjunct of community life, citizen participation. The nature of citizen participation must be understood from the outset. Bridgewater's citizens were encouraged to hold extremely high expectations for their involvement in the Citizens' Planning Council. These expectations exceeded the practical and had to be reduced by a Council which came to realize the importance of asserting its own role as the final decision making authority in the community. Unfortunately, the Council does not appear to have realized a parallel need to tackle the problem of citizen participation at the very early stage of local government decision making.

On balance Bridgewater's experience with development has been a fairly happy one. As will be seen, compared with Port Hawkesbury, Bridgewater has been wildly successful in adapting to the importation of a major new industry. For Port Hawkesbury development has meant that schools were severely overcrowded; inadequate medical services were rendered totally unsatisfactory; social problems abounded; and town indebtedness reached unacceptable levels. The striking difference between this experience and Bridgewater's is illustrated by the pattern of discussion of the two towns. In the following chapter the reader will search unsuccessfully for an extended discussion of experiments in citizen participation in the planning process, not because Port Hawkesbury neglected this aspect of development - in fact, the town had some notable successes - but because local initiative was repeatedly negated and overshadowed by the decisions of government and corporate bureaucrats. In consequence the Port Hawkesbury community has come to feel that its future depends either on remote, inscrutable economic forces or upon the whims of politicians and bureaucrats in Halifax.

Bridgewater has experienced some of Port Hawkesbury's afflictions, most notably in negotiations with the Community Planning Division and the Departments of Education and Highways. But for the most part the community has been able to retain a sense of controlling its own development pattern and it has been able to keep alive a confidence in its own spirit of enterprise. We can attribute this to five factors:

1. The population of Bridgewater (4,755 in 1966 and 5,231 in 1971) and of its catchment area (30,000 to 50,000)[33] was large enough to absorb without undue disruption the population increase caused by the creation of 1,200 new jobs at Michelin. Simply in terms of ratio of old to new residents, the previously existing community would not be overwhelmed by a bloc of newcomers importing a variety of unaccustomed needs and life styles. Other characteristics of the population are even more important, however. Throughout the fairly lengthy history of Lunenburg-Queens the region has enjoyed a

stable population base. In 1901, for example, Lunenburg County had 32,389 inhabitants. Over the next forty years the population fluctuated within 1,500 of that figure, not rising to 34,998 until 1961 and 38,422 in 1971. This stability has given the region a close-knit web of family connections supplemented by an extensive network of community groups. Together these have created a stable social fabric capable of integrating a population influx far larger than that brought by Michelin.[34]

2. The Bridgewater area has existed as a community for well over a century. A number of towns and villages in the region have existed for more than two hundred years. They have seen distressing poverty, but also great prosperity, and in so doing have accumulated an "inventory" of public utilities and community facilities - such as roads, bridges, schools, churches, halls, parks, gymnasia, and swimming pools - that required only piecemeal expansion to meet the demands of recent additions to the population. Similarly the provision of social, medical, and recreational services could be expanded marginally as changes in demand occurred. Only in the need for expanded educational facilities and major improvement in Bridgewater's transportation system is there any pressure comparable to that to be observed in Port Hawkesbury.

3. The Community, through its civic leaders, the business community, and its professional advisors, demonstrated the flexibility and foresight to switch its development strategy from one of seeking out opportunities for expansion to one of anticipating the effects of development. Of the development activities within the town's control, the decision to create the Industrial Development Commission was undoubtedly the most important factor leading to an attempt at orderly change or planning. The Commission was the institutionalization of a role traditionally played by the business community. In perceiving the need for planning and for social development, it legitimized activities that are not always readily accepted by conservative communities on the verge of expansion. By its existence, it drew attention to the need for a more popularly based planning group, and, although that need has been met only partially, it is likely that the present organization provides a base for more effective public participation in future. Bridgewater was also extremely fortunate in achieving a good working relationship with neighbouring local governments, notably through the establishment and operation of the District Planning Commission.

4. Through good fortune as well as good judgment Bridgewater obtained a major industry compatible with the town's physical and

cultural environment. Michelin's use of water resources has caused concern, but in other respects its physical plant is not obtrusive. In these respects Michelin conforms to the criteria established by the IDC when it began the search for industrial development. In other respects, Bridgewater's experience with a multinational corporation has been unusually felicitous. Michelin's paternalistic policies arouse the fury of labour leaders, but the company's stability and the care with which it maintains cordial relations with the town have undoubtedly eased its assimilation into the community.

5. Finally, Bridgewater has been fortunate in not being designated a major growth centre. Desirable though such designation is sometimes considered, it has the effect of transferring virtually all aspects of local control of development to senior levels of government and to major corporations. Because it is seen primarily as a provincial regional centre, Bridgewater has escaped the gross interference in its affairs that will be observed in Port Hawkesbury. Probably, too, Bridgewater's freedom has been enhanced by Michelin's clearcut policies concerning its relations with host communities. Though sometimes inappropriate in North America, these may have assisted Bridgewater to avoid becoming entangled in a maze of development task forces and programs organized by senior levels of government to supervise the development process. An absence of interference from other governments may also be attributable to the fact that, except in the Michelin case, Bridgewater's expansion was commercial, rather than industrial. Expansion decisions in the commercial field tend, relatively speaking, to be "micro-decisions" not the large scale internationally oriented decisions that result in the building of large manufacturing plants or heavy industry. Although in aggregate commercial decisions may profoundly affect a region, their local orientation and small scale place them outside the sphere of interest of senior levels of government and make them amenable to control by local authorities.

Many other factors have contributed to the fact that the Bridgewater area has assimilated major expansion with relative ease and with a considerable degree of local control; for example, the pre-existence of a diverse and relatively sound economic base. But these five elements - a stable community populous enough to absorb a major influx of new residents; adequate community services; competent leadership; a form of expansion compatible with the existing environment of the community; and minimum entanglement with senior levels of government - must be seen as the major factors promoting orderly expansion and a considerable degree of local initiative in the planning process.

Figure 2

STRAIT OF CANSO REGION

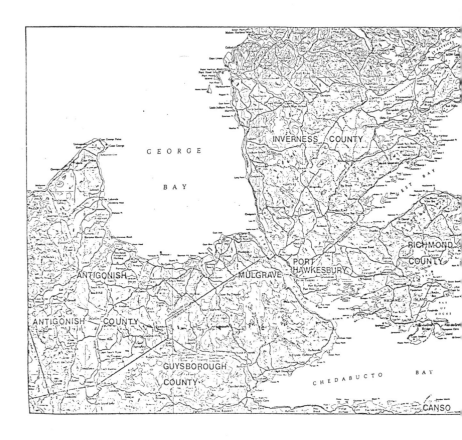

Source: *Terms of Reference for Port Hastings - Port Hawkesbury - Point Tupper Development Plan* (draft, April 22, 1974, mimeo.), pp. 9-10.

III. PORT HAWKESBURY: DEVELOPMENT AND DEPENDENCE

The Pattern of Industrial Development

By the mid-1950s, the Town of Port Hawkesbury urgently needed industrial development. An established fishing community, the town for many years had supplemented this staple, but marginal, industry with the provision of transportation services between Cape Breton Island and the mainland. A number of ferries crossed the Strait of Canso daily, carrying railway cars as well as road vehicles. With the official start of construction on the Canso Causeway in 1953, this important feature of the local economy was destined to disappear. The outlook for the town was bleak. Never prosperous, the demise of one of two staple industries spelt imminent poverty. There appeared to be no alternative industry willing to move in. Even the extensive forest-resource on its doorstep seemed to be unwanted. A 1.2 million acre tract of crown land known as the Oxford Leasehold had had to be repossessed by the Province when the Oxford Pulp and Paper Company failed to establish a viable operation, and no other company had appeared to take Oxford's place. A succession of appeals to government brought little response and, on one occasion at least, a delegation from the town to the Minister of Trade and Industry was "laughed out of the Minister's office".[1] With no skilled workmen in the area, limited natural resources, an extremely unsatisfactory water supply situation, and a weak regional economy, Halifax's assessment seemed to be a correct one.

Nevertheless, members of the local community established, in 1954, an organization known as the Four Counties Development Association. Headed by community leaders, and in particular, by the manager of the Port Hawkesbury branch of the Royal Bank of Canada, the Association worked primarily to establish a pulp mill, an industry logically related to the region's resources as they were perceived at that time. Fifteen years later their efforts were credited with being of crucial importance to the development of the Strait area.

> At a most decisive time, in the Strait area, this Development Association established a climate receptive of change, an atmosphere charged with realistic optimism, rather than despair, an attitude that said that the people of the Strait area can develop the ground-work for a prosperous economy, indeed, a very stable one.[2]

Their work did give an important boost to morale in the region, but - as has happened so often in the recent history of the Strait - development took place because of factors over which the local community had no control. During 1956 and 1957 these overriding factors were the availability of the Oxford lease and recognition, by government and industry, of the potential of the harbour created by the Causeway.

In the summer of 1956, scarcely a year after the opening of the Causeway, the Stora Kopparberg Company of Sweden opened correspondence with the Nova Scotia government, suggesting that the company carry out a survey of the province to establish whether or not it was feasible to build a pulp mill in Nova Scotia. In the fall of 1956 the company carried out the survey and by November 1957 had selected a site at Point Tupper. They asked the government to guarantee sufficient quantities of water to the proposed new plant, which was to cost $40,000,000 and was expected to have an annual production capacity of 125,000 tons of high grade bleached chemical pulp to be used for the manufacture of fine paper, tissue, food containers, and other paper products.[3]

The mill's water requirements were met by tapping a series of lakes some distance from Point Tupper. At the same time, the Four Counties Development Association carried out a program of organizing woodlot owners for the purpose of providing a planned long-range program designed to ensure adequate pulpwood supplies and reserves for the proposed mill. In July 1959 the province expropriated 6,000 acres of land at Point Tupper for an industrial park and provided a site there for the chemical pulp mill.

The Stora Kopparberg mills, under the name of Nova Scotia Pulp Limited*, began operations in 1962, and by 1970 the company had invested approximately $133 million in the area. Annual production was running at about 130,000 tons of bleached pulp and 160,000 tons of newsprint, with an average employment of around 800.[4]

Of the two factors that revolutionized the Strait economy, the availabiltiy of the Oxford lease undoubtedly had the greatest influence on the Stora Kopparberg decision. As far as other development decisions were concerned, however, recognition of the Strait's potential as a port was far more important.

The harbour's unusual depth had long been appreciated, but it was the unexpected consequence of completion of the Causeway, together with major changes in shipping technology, that gave the harbour its unique potential and made it the keystone of development in the Strait region. Briefly, that potential was first recognized during the winter of 1955 when the people of Port Hawkesbury realized that they were

*Later, Nova Scotia Forest Industries. The company was 80 per cent owned by Stora Kopparberg Bergslags-Aktrebelag and 20 per cent by Scott Paper Company of Philadephia. Stora Kopparberg acquired Scott's interest on October 31, 1969.

living beside an ice-free harbour, one of the deepest on the eastern part of the continent and one of the few in the world capable of berthing the large freighters and oil carriers then beginning to come into service. Once this fact became widely appreciated the problem of selling Port Hawkesbury as an industrial site greatly diminished and gave way to the problems of adjusting to a total change in the region's economy.

During the initial stages of development at the Strait - what some members of the community refer to as "Boom One" and officialdom as "Phase One" of the development cycle* - construction of the pulp mill dominated the local economy. But the role of the harbour was becoming significant. Between 1956 and 1963, the area witnessed the acquisition by the British-American Oil Company (later part of the Gulf Oil Company) of 2,300 acres for a refinery and the construction of a major docking facility by the Bestwall Gypsum Company, a subsidary of Georgia Pacific, which mines over 600,000 tons of gypsum annually at River Denys for manufacture in the United States. The Province designated Point Tupper as an industrial park for heavy industry and began promoting the Strait region as a major site for industrial development.

During Boom One and the lull in activity that followed, from 1963 to 1966, initial contact was made between the Province and the companies whose entry into the area precipitated Boom Two. B / A - Gulf's interest has already been mentioned. In February 1966 the Province first communicated with the Canadian General Electric Company, which was interested in establishing a heavy water plant in Nova Scotia, and two years later, in June of 1968, the government and the company announced that a $75 million plant would be built. The plant was completed in mid-1970, with actual production scheduled for later that year. It was to employ 140 people. Associated with the CGE construction was the building by the Nova Scotia Power Commission of a $20,000,000 facility at Point Tupper. Simultaneously the Gulf Oil Company began building its $88 million oil refinery and, at the height of construction (mid-1970), employed a labour force of 1,700 men. The plant was designed to employ about 150 when fully operational. As well, the federal government undertook to construct as $17,000,000 deepwater terminal for the company on the Point Tupper site. The facility was designed to handle the world's largest oil cargo vessels. In all, $400 million was invested in heavy industry at Point Tupper.

Once in operation, the new companies began to make their long-term effects felt. As Table 2 shows, employment in manufacturing activity in Richmond and Inverness counties nearly doubled between 1966 and 1971, almost exclusively as a result of the

*See Table 1 for a summary of development activity.

Table 1

SEQUENCE OF INDUSTRIAL DEVELOPMENT
POINT TUPPER, 1953-1975

1953	Start of construction of Canso Causeway.
1955	Causeway completed.
1956	Stora Kopparberg investigates pulp mill potential in Nova Scotia.
1957	Stora Kopparberg selects Point Tupper site.
1959	Province expropriates site for Point Tupper Industrial Park.
	Stora Kopparberg mill under construction.
1960	BA Oil (Gulf) begins purchase of 2,300 acres for refinery at Point Tupper.
1961	Docking facilities for Bestwall Gypsum under construction.
1962	Bestwall dock in operation.
	Stora Kopparberg mill in operation.
	End of 'Boom One'.
1963 to 1966	Lull in construction brings local recession.
1968	CGE heavy water plant under construction.
	N.S. Power Commission plant under construction.
1969	Stora Kopparberg expansion launched to increase pulp production and introduce newsprint mill.
	Construction of Gulf oil refinery begins.
	Construction of federal government wharf for refinery begins.
1970	CGE plant completed.
	NSPC plant completed.
	Expansion of NSPC plant announced.
1971	Stora Kopparberg expansion completed.
	Gulf Oil refinery completed.
1973	NSPC expansion completed.
	End of 'Boom Two', and beginning of second local recession.
	Focus of development interest shifts to Melford, near Mulgrave, where provincial governments hopes to locate at least one additional refinery.
1975	Talk of these projects and related petrochemical complex dies down as world-wide recession deepens.

Table 2

PRINCIPAL STATISTICS FOR MANUFACTURING INDUSTRIES
RICHMOND AND INVERNESS COUNTIES, 1966-1971

		Manufacturing Activity								Total Activity		
		Production & Related Workers		Man hours	Wages	Cost of fuel & elec-	Cost of materials & sup-	Value of shipments of goods of own	Value added manufac-	Total Employees	Salaries and	Value added total
Year	Estab-lish-ments	Male	Female	paid '000	$'000	tricity $'000	plies used $'000	manufacture $'000	turing activity $'000	Number	Wages $'000	activity $'000
1966	25	660	150	1,728	3,322	890	13,317	22,540	8,338	1,007	4,593	8,319
1967	27	615	148	1,768	3,294	851	12,486	19,351	6,165	981	4,817	6,161
1968	21	806		1,722	3,480	862	13,388	20,658	6,179	1,035	5,121	6,250
1969	23	872		1,910	4,297	875	14,119	24,011	8,877	1,101	6,030	8,914
1970	21	738		1,663	4,350	1,100	14,137	23,623	8,820	984	6,440	8,857
1971	22	1,053		2,241	7,555	5,989	49,565	44,558	-5,923	1,473	12,426	-5,873

Source: Nova Scotia Department of Development, *County Profile: Richmond* (Halifax: 1974); and derived there from Statistics Canada census data, 1966-1971.

Table 3

POPULATION TRENDS, PORT HAWKESBURY AND ADJACENT AREAS
(CENSUS DISTRICT 'C', INVERNESS COUNTY; DISTRICTS "A" AND "C", RICHMOND COUNTY)

	Total	Pre-School 0-4	School Age 5-9	School Age 10-14	Labour Force Age (15-64) 15-19	20-24	25-34	35-44	45-54	55-64	Pension Age 65-69	70
1951												
Port Hawkesbury	1034	141	109	86	90	68	122	141	86	92	32	67
Inverness 'C'	3121	343	333	265	256	154	321	397	285	264	159	344
Richmond 'A'	3894	566	478	413	318	245	441	443	311	259	132	288
Richmond 'C'	3825	512	455	328	304	221	486	442	332	307	158	280
	11874	1562	1375	1092	968	688	1370	1423	1014	922	481	979
1961												
Port Hawkesbury	1346	190	189	136	102	70	175	151	126	82	39	86
Inverness 'C'	3375	393	347	395	322	189	297	337	396	275	126	298
Richmond 'A'	4242	569	515	521	377	271	459	412	411	275	137	295
Richmond 'C'	4317	529	528	505	410	228	457	510	412	299	150	289
	13280	1681	1579	1557	1211	758	1388	1410	1345	931	452	968
1971												
Port Hawkesbury	3375	395	430	380	335	330	525	375	295	170	50	85
Inverness 'C'	4155	470	480	455	375	345	555	390	325	340	135	285
Richmond 'A'	4935	520	610	600	530	395	595	440	405	380	150	305
Richmond 'C'	4965	555	625	565	520	370	555	440	495	390	140	305
	17430	1940	2145	2000	1760	1440	2230	1645	1520	1280	475	980

Source: Graham, Napier, Hébert and Associates Ltd., Project 3.9: Junior-Senior High School and Associated Community Facilities, Port Hawkesbury, Nova Scotia: Report II. Vol. I: Complete Project Information

Point Tupper concerns. They are now said to employ 1,200 workers.[5] Population, reversing a fifty-year downward trend in the area around Port Hawkesbury, increased from 11,874 in 1951 to 17,430 in 1971.* The proportion of the population of labour force age rose from 53.8 per cent to 56.7 per cent in the same period (Tables 3 and 4). Wages also rose, so that by 1972 Port Hawkesbury income tax returns averaged $7,445, the highest average in the province.[6]

Table 4

**POPULATION OF LABOUR FORCE AGE IN PORT HAWKESBURY
AND ADJACENT AREAS OF RICHMOND AND
INVERNESS COUNTIES**

Year	Population of Labour Force Age (15-64)	Percentage of Total Population
1951	6,385	53.8
1961	7,043	53.0
1971	9,875	56.7

Source: Graham, Napier, Hébert and Associates Ltd., *Project 3.9: Junior-Senior High School and Associated Community Facilities, Port Hawkesbury, Nova Scotia,* Report II: Volume I: *Complete Project Information* (1973), Section 3, Demographic Data / Census Data.

The peak of development activity was reached in 1970, although the 1973 completion of the Nova Scotia Power Corporation's expansion at Point Tupper actually marks the end of 'Boom Two'. Since that time Point Tupper and Port Hawkesbury have given place to Mulgrave as the focal point for expansionist rhetoric. Efforts have been made to attract new refineries to the Mulgrave location, and much has been said of the prospects for a petrochemical complex. In the uncertain economic conditions of the current period, however, few firm investment decisions have been taken, and the region has slowly adjusted to the fact that for the next few years at least development is a thing of the past.

Although these few paragraphs and the summary presented in Table 1 provide only a cursory view of a dramatic cycle of development at Point Tupper, they do give some idea of the sweep of events that engulfed neighbouring Port Hawkesbury. Notably they emphasize first, the scale of the forces at work in the Strait area, and second, the fact that industrial development occurred because the international

*These figures refer only to the area around Port Hawkesbury on the Cape Breton side of the Canso Causeway. They assume that the causeway, with its toll, represents a barrier to complete social and economic integration of the region. If this barrier is ignored, the regional population (considered as lying within a 30-mile radius of the Strait) amounted to 32,700 (Nova Scotia Department of Municipal Affairs Community Planning Division, *Strait of Canso Regional Development Plan* (Halifax: 1967), p. 18.

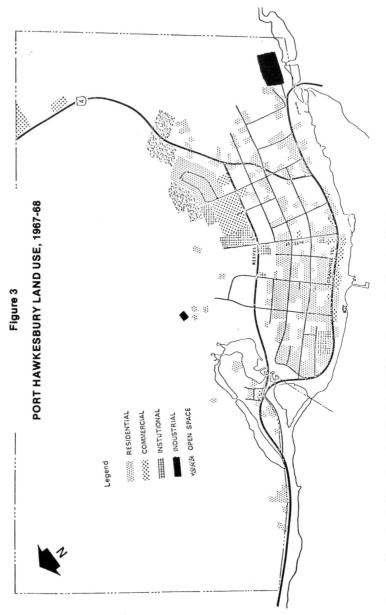

Figure 3

PORT HAWKESBURY LAND USE, 1967-68

Legend

RESIDENTIAL
COMMERCIAL
INSTUTIONAL
INDUSTRIAL
OPEN SPACE

Source: Nova Scotia Department of Municipal Affairs, Community Planning Division, *Proposed Port Hawkesbury Development Plan* (Halifax: 1968).

36

business conditions which now make the Strait a viable industrial location were well beyond the influence of local government and to an extent beyond that of senior governments. These two aspects of industrial development - its scale and its dependence on apparently uncontrollable forces - have dominated every effort made by the Strait communities to adjust to their changed economies and to obtain for themselves some of improvement in living conditions that was promised as each new sod was turned and each new plant opened. Nowhere has this dominance, and the concomitant frustration of local initiative, been demonstrated more strikingly than at Port Hawkesbury.

The Social Consequences of Development
Point Tupper's expansion took Port Hawkesbury by surprise.

[The town]was unprepared to cope with the sudden influx of a large construction work force. Land and housing prices rose sharply, accommodation was scarce and expensive. The Town's municipal services were totally inadequate to meet the demands of incoming population. School facilities were insufficient and additional temporary quarters had to be provided. There were no by-laws governing private home construction or the establishment of trailer parks and 'instant' communities sprang up in areas where there were no water or sewage facilities. Ribbon development began to spread along the paved highways leading away from the area, adding to the Town's problem of providing services.[7]

The town's centre of gravity shifted away from its traditional base on Granville Street to what was to become a four-lane highway (Reeves Street) which feeds industrial traffic to Point Tupper and serves as the main highway to Louisdale and Sydney (See Map, Figure 3). Along this highway were built, during the early and mid 1960s a new combined high school and elementary school, two shopping centres, motels, churches, and several other commercial and civic services. Two new subdivisions were developed at this time, one in the north end of town (Hawkesbury Heights), and the other (Summit Park) forming part of the cluster of new buildings around Reeves Street. In the old business district, new bank facilities and a federal building were built, as well as a new tavern. From its 1951 figure of 1,034 the town's population grew to 1,346 by 1961 and 1,866 by 1966. In retrospect, in the view of a later provincial Minister of Development, "the initial transition to an industrial-based economy moved rather smoothly, especially when considered in relation to the experiences encountered during the recent (1968-71) heavy growth period."[8]

The passage of time and the local inter-boom recession no doubt coloured this assessment. For the residents of the area, the first boom and its aftermath frequently brought grave problems:

With the pulp mill completed and the announced oil refinery postponed indefinitely, the area experienced a period of great uncertainty. Although overall employment in the area had tripled in the period 1950-1964, many of those employed were 'newcomers' to the area - construction workers who had remained to take permanent jobs at the new mill or administrative and technical people who had come into the area from other parts of Canada. The original residents were still suffering from unemployment. . . . Many of these people were older citizens who were not qualified to accept employment in the new industries. They lacked the necessary technical skills required and retraining programs were not available to them.

As the main body of construction workers left the area, the service industries declined and retail trade fell off. However, the cost of living remained high - based falsely on the economic conditions which prevailed during the period of construction. Permanent housing was still scarce and very costly. Land prices inflated and taxes rose . . . .

The enthusiasm that had prevailed during the initial period of development had disappeared. Many of the area's residents were disappointed by the events that had taken place. They believed they had been 'taken in' by the promises of government and industry. They felt that a few large industries had invaded their area, causing changes in their traditional life style without consulting them, and had, in the end, resulted in more costs than benefits to the area. Their attitude toward further development was one of hostility and suspicion.9

The experience of Boom One, sobering though it was, proved insignificant in contrast to its successor. In terms of financial outlay and demand for skilled labour, Boom Two's impact on the local community was overwhelming.

During 1970 and 1971, Point Tupper's industrial construction labour force was maintained at around the 3,000 mark. In addition, construction of infrastructure at the industrial park, expansion of provincial and municipal public services, and residential and small business construction, together with expansion of the permanent labour force, created a roistering, brawling frontier town out of what had been, ten years before, a small, traditional community. For one local minister, it was "unbelievable":

Overnight this town tripled in size, with construction workers who had all kinds of money. They just had money to burn! They could light cigarettes with $5 bills and never feel the money going. They were making queues in front of the Liquor Commission every day. There is a man in town . . . who bought himself a truck and rebuilt his home and modeled his home over again, just on the money he raised by going into the job sites every day and picking up the old beer bottles. . . .While I was here, in 1969, a bunch of construction workers got six teenage girls and passed them around through the construction camps, and it took a big crew of Mounties to go in and get them out. Of the construction workers who were here in 1969, 300 of them had criminal records. I don't hold a record against a man, but it gives you an idea of the people who were here . . . . The crew had no roots at all. No control. Didn't give a sweet damn about the community or the people in it.10

The construction camps, their violence and lawlessness, together with the labour problems that plagued construction of the Point

Tupper industries, were temporary. They had some continuing effect, but soon became a memory. On the other hand, the permanent employees of the industries that now started production had to be provided for on a long-term basis. They wanted a more stable community and, as at least one study had warned,[11] they needed sophisticated social services. Port Hawkesbury, which by 1971 was at the centre of a population of 17,430 and had itself grown to 3,427, a 140 per cent increase over its 1961 population, felt that it would bear the brunt of this demand for services:

> As the principal organized community in proximity to the new industrial area, the Town of Port Hawkesbury attracted a large population of [new permanent employees]. It should be noted, however, that it is not only a numerical increase. The new citizens are generally much more urbanized than the original population, and as a consequence have brought with them much greater dependence upon and expectation of what services are required from municipal government.12

Expansion meant that the demand for services changed in three ways. First, the scale of existing services had to be increased considerably; then a much greater variety of services had to be provided; finally, the particular situation at the Strait placed unusually heavy demands on certain types of services.

As one would expect, the most immediate and obvious effects of expansion were associated with changes in the scale of education services. The principal of the Port Hawkesbury Elementary School noted:

> Our biggest problem is overcrowding. We don't have Phys. Ed. because we don't have a specialist teacher, but even if we did, there is very little a teacher can do outside the classroom. When I came, the gym was available for Phys.Ed. And we don't have a library. We have our books out in the hallway, and we have books within the classroom. To me the most pressing need is for a large room to be used as a library. And for the gym to be used as a gym.13

Similar problems were noted elsewhere, along with high student-teacher ratios and the difficulty of planning for school populations that fluctuated considerably.[14]

The strain on educational facilities was only one of the most prominent features of rapid growth. Medical facilities in western Cape Breton had not been developed with an eye to expansion at the Strait, and when growth did take place in that area the lack of appropriately located health services soon came to be seen as a major problem. In particular, the need for hospital services became, and still is, a burning issue. Inverness County is equipped with three small general hospitals, two at Inverness, 60 miles from Port Hawkesbury, and the third at Cheticamp, about 100 miles away. Together they provide approximately 100 beds. Richmond County's hospital at Arichat is closer, but is so small that even the province's Department of

Development considers it "far from adequate".[15] It is equipped with 14 beds and cribs. For Port Hawkesbury residents the only alternatives to these small hospitals are in Antigonish, nearly forty miles away, and Sydney, about 100 miles distant. These last hospitals are referral centres expected to serve all of northeastern Nova Scotia and Cape Breton Island.

Other medical services are under similar pressure. Nursing homes and homes for the elderly are no more numerous than the hospitals and no more conveniently located. In 1974 doctor-patient ratios were reported at 1:1,600 in Inverness County[16] and at 1:2,546 in Richmond.[17] The provincial average is 1:697.[18] A local service club in Port Hawkesbury organized clinics serviced by specialists from Halifax, but these were no substitute for a permanent, properly equipped facility staffed by full time and visiting professionals.[19] The ratio of dentists to patients in Inverness is 1:10,000,[20] and in Richmond, 1:12,734.[21]

Social services also reflected expanded needs. In addition to the Department of Public Welfare's Social Assistance Program and the Children's Aid Program, Port Hawkesbury in the 1960s was served by school counselling services.[22] By 1970 the need for family counselling had led to the opening of a Port Hawkesbury office of the Family Services of Eastern Nova Scotia, an agency sponsored by the Roman Catholic Diocese of Antigonish and supported by diocesan and government grants.[23] Two years later the town of Port Hawkesbury appointed a welfare officer of its own. A further indication of the scale of demand for social services was given by one of the Family Service workers, who reported that he and his two colleagues managed a load of 425 cases in 1972, almost three times the caseload at his previous agency.[24]

Supplementing official and semi-official agencies were the town's five religious institutions. The Catholic church, the traditional church in the community, provided space for the Family Services agency and an eye specialist, whilst the Catholic priest and the United Church, Anglican, and Pentecostal ministers engaged in various types of counselling. The church buildings themselves - three of them built during the boom years - were in steady demand as meeting places for community groups.[25] By 1973 these latter numbered about forty, most of them requiring meeting places and some of them, specialized recreational facilities.

In general recreational facilities were either non-existent or quickly outgrown. "They complain about kids playing on the street, and say they should be playing on the church yards and school yards [commented one minister]. But how many church yards and school yards do we have? . . . Playgrounds in the town are next to nil. There are a couple of swings by the arena, and that's about it."[26] Skaters found ice-time hard to come by at the Strait of Canso Community

Recreation Centre, a building erected in 1963 and used for bingo, wrestling, shows, and dances as well as for skating and hockey. A two-sheet curling club built in 1965 was used to capacity by 1973. Club members felt that a doubling of capacity would meet that year's demand. Three of the four schools in the town had gyms by 1973, but one had been taken over for classroom use and the use of the others was limited by poor acoustics, lack of facilities for adults, and the educational priorities of the schools themselves. A bowling alley and ancient frame movie house provided the only commercial recreation facilities. Library services were delivered by bookmobile operating out of a branch library established at Mulgrave in 1969.[27]

Coupled with the surge in demand for medical and social services and recreational and education facilities was a need for accomodation and an increased pressure for various public utilities. Between 1967 and 1973 the town issued building permits for 745 new dwelling units, and approximately $4 million worth of industrial, commercial, and government construction (see Table 5). The Four Counties Development Association had warned at the beginning of Boom One that a reliable water supply, sewers, paved streets, and serviced building sites were all needed to meet industrial development. The reliable water supply had become an urgent necessity during Boom One, and the need for sewers, a sewage treatment plant, sidewalks, paved roads, and street lighting was evident as Boom Two began. By 1973 the town, estimated at that time to have a population of approximately 4,000, had acquired a debt load of $6.7 million as a result of meeting these needs and the costs of building new educational facilities.[28] Taxes had risen accordingly, so that the average tax per household in Port Hawkesbury was one of the highest in the province,[29] contributing to the fact that rents in the town were the highest in the province in 1971.[30]

While the scale of change in demand for public services is an outstanding feature of the growth problem faced by Port Hawkesbury and neighbouring communities, it is probably less difficult to deal with than the required diversification of services. A simple increment in demand for a few services can usually be provided for merely by adding to staff or facilities. Some economies of scale can even be achieved. The provision of increasingly diverse services is much more difficult to attain, particularly when those segments of the population requiring such services are not large enough to fully sustain them.

Newcomers to Port Hawkesbury represented a wide variety of backgrounds. One educator found his school had become "a miniature United Nations. We have children from all over the world, speaking many languages."[31] Their parents pursued a variety of occupations, ranging from construction work to the professional and managerial. Many placed highly sophisticated demands on the community's social services.

Table 5

BUILDING PERMITS ISSUED, PORT HAWKESBURY*
1967-1973

Number of Dwelling Units

Year	Single Dwellings	Double Dwellings	Apartments	Conversions	Total
1973	57	--	26	1	84
1972	28	4	--	--	32
1971	51	2	--	--	53
1970	108	2	24	3	137
1969	32	4	205	--	241
1968	26	4	86	3	119
1967	16	10	60	1	87

Value of Residential and Non-Residential Construction ($'000)

Year	New Residential	Repair Residential	Residential Total	Industrial	Com-mercial	Institution & Goverment	Total
1973	--	--	1,821	20	60	80	1,981
1972			650	14	524	397	1,585
1971	981	39	1,020	--	297	92	1,409
1970	2,291	34	2,325	125	263	935	3,648
1969	3,376	17	3,393	--	1,248	--	4,641
1968	1,287	29	1,316	14	197	--	1,527
1967	959	2	916	50	82	--	1,093

*Only area in the county which requires building permits.

Source: Nova Scotia Department of Development, *County Profile: Inverness* (Halifax:1974), Table 43, p. 117.

An indication of their range can be obtained from a 1973 feasibility study for a school and community centre complex, which paints a fascinating portrait of the town at that time.[32] A prominent concern was the lack of medical facilities, but the paucity of educational facilities and specialized social services was a recurrent complaint of community leaders and citizens at large. When asked to indicate which community facilities they most desired in the proposed complex, a random sample of residents gave priority to a public library, swimming pool, gymnasium, and ice rink, but teenager drop-in centres, children's playgrounds, outdoor sports facilities, a movie theatre, bookstore, and restaurants were also considered important. Although ambitious objectives for a still small community - even one serving a hinterland three times its size - these services were common enough in the urban centres from which many of Point Tupper's new employees came.

An interesting illustration of the intensity with which newcomers desired such urban oriented facilities is provided by Table 6, which contrasts the priority index ratios* of those surveyed during the 1973 study. Although all groups ranked the public library, the movie theatre, and facilities for public swimming at the top of their list of priorities, those who were new arrivals or who had lived in the area for less than four years desired these facilities with a much greater intensity than those who had been resident for longer periods. The absence of these sorts of facilities, according to a report sponsored by BA / Gulf, was one of the factors contributing to "a high turnover . . . in industrial personnel at Point Tupper."[33]

Just as Port Hawkesbury experienced a demand for an enlarged scale of services and a broadening of their range, so the town found itself meeting problems generated by the particular conditions of the region's expansion. Of these the problem of integrating the individual in the community was the most pressing. It was at the heart of a number of particularly intransigent social difficulties.

Although we know that Port Hawkesbury's population nearly tripled in the twenty years following 1951, our knowledge of precisely how many newcomers the town absorbed in that period is very limited. The 1973 survey suggests that nearly fifty per cent of the population in and around the town had lived there less than twelve years. For some of these newcomers the community was an ideal spot, particularly for a young family. They enjoyed living in the town, found many friends there for themselves and their families, and came to speak warmly of the community. For a number of others, however, Port Hawkesbury was a trap in which the lack of social amenities and the area's poor physical planning exacerbated the loneliness that naturally follows the move to a new town. Their needs were apparent, particularly to religious leaders in the community, one of whom considered that

---

*The survey approached approximately 1 out of every 7 students in the Port Hawkesbury area; 1 out of every 15 students in the outlying areas; 1 out of every 6 households in Port Hawkesbury area; 1 out of every 15 in outlying areas except for Isle Madame-St. Peters, where 1 out of every 50 households was approached. Of 594 people approached 92 per cent responded.

The priority index ratio referred to here is calculated as:

$$\text{PIR 1} = \frac{(\% \text{ response who would personally use the item}) - (\% \text{ response who feel the item is not important to include})}{(\% \text{ number of possible responses}) - (\text{sum of two top figures})}$$

To quote the study, the "priority index ratio becomes larger as more people indicated they would use the item or as few people indicated they did not feel it was important to include in the centre. [It] thus forms a representative indication of priority demand for an item. The priority index ratios are an adequate indication of community attitude towards both potential use and importance of the centre, since in most cases there was a direct correlation to personally using the centre and to the importance attached to it." Graham, Napier, Hébert and Associates Ltd., *Project 3.9: Junior-Senior High School and Associated Community Facilities, Port Hawkesbury, Nova Scotia, Report II*, Volume I: *Complete Project Information (1973), p. 434.*

Table 6

PRIORITY INDEX RATIOS BY LENGTH OF RESIDENCE IN THE PORT HAWKESBURY AREA, SHOWING INTENSITY OF DEMAND FOR COMMUNITY SERVICES

Residence Less Than 1 Year		Residence 1-3 Years	
Public Library	7.00	Movie Theatre	6.57
Movie Theatre	4.33	Swimming Pool	4.91
Swimming Pool	3.75	Public Library	4.25
Public Swimming	3.75	Shopping Centre	3.43
Book Store	3.29	Large Restaurant	3.30
Shopping Centre	3.00	Public swimming	3.23
Public Skating	3.00	Clothing Store	2.89
Gymnasium	2.17	Sidewalk Restaurant	2.42
Large Restaurant	2.14	Gymnasium	2.25
Ice Rink	2.00	Coffee Shop / Cafe	2.19
Outdoor swimming	1.80	Theatre	2.00
Theatre	1.73	Record Shop	1.90
Coffee Shop / Cafe	1.46	Book Store	1.85
Doctor's Office	1.44	Doctor's Office	1.61
Dance Hall	1.44	Outdoor swimming	1.39
Clothing Store	1.44	Dance Hall	1.39
Bus trips out of area	1.29	Dental Office	1.39
Record Shop	1.25	Community Park	1.33
Keep fit	1.11	Public skating	1.27
Tennis Courts	1.00	Swim classes	1.25

Residence 4-12 Years		Residence More Than 12 Years	
Public swimming	3.46	Public Library	2.56
Movie Theatre	3.40	Movie Theatre	1.93
Swimming Pool	3.38	Swimming Pool	1.90
Public Library	3.10	Clothing Store	1.79
Theatre	2.78	Public swimming	1.75
Clothing Store	2.03	Shopping Centre	1.62
Gymnasium	1.96	Theatre	1.59
Shopping Centre	1.85	Dance Hall	1.44
Public skating	1.81	Coffee Shop / Cafe	1.35
Coffee Shop / Cafe	1.71	Dental Office	1.32
Record Shop	1.36	Book Store	1.27
Community Park	1.33	Public skating	1.23
Book Store	1.28	Large Restaurant	1.18
Ice Rink	1.25	Doctor's Office	1.10
Keep fit	1.24	Gymnasium	1.07
Doctor's Office	1.24	Record Shop	.97
Dental Office	1.20	Community Park	.95
Dance Hall	1.19	Outdoor swimming	.95
Large Restaurant	1.15	Ice Rink	.95
Badminton	1.14	Swim classes	.84

Source: Priority Index Ratios, Graham, Napier, Hébert and Associates Ltd., *Project 3.9 Junior-Senior High School and Associated Community Facilities, Port Hawkesbury Nova Scotia,* Report II, Volume I: *Complete Report Information* (1973), pp. 434ff.

. . . the greatest difficulty and problem that I find in this community is loneliness. People feel alienated from the community. They feel frustrated, in that they can't seem to participate in it. There is a lot of anger and resentment towards this community. A lot of people have been moved here, not at their request, but at their company's command. If you want to work for us, you're going to work in Hawkesbury! This sets up a great deal of resentment against the community.[34]

Service clubs and other community groups had difficulty maintaining stable memberships, difficulties that were increased by the lack of adequate and permanent facilities in which to meet.[35] Potential leaders of such groups lived in the community, but could not be persuaded to join. Those who did take part moved on to other jobs. Not surprisingly their commitment to the group and to the community was limited, a reportedly common characteristic in the area.[36] In short a stable social fabric was absent in the community. This affected the wives and children of the employees of the new industries most acutely:

The husband has his job, his pay cheque, and his confreres at work. The wife has nobody . . . . The kids, because their families don't, they don't have roots. They are lost to find reasonable sorts of ways to become integrated.[37]

Alcoholism was equally symptomatic of the community's instability. One social worker, describing its incidence as "phenomenal", claimed that 40 per cent of his caseload was related to drinking problems.[38] Family disintegration, alcoholism, and the many other problems associated with this sort of dislocation added considerably to the burden of social services provided by the community and the province.

In the spring of 1968 the Community Planning Division of the Department of Municipal Affairs urged the people of Port Hawkesbury to adopt a community development plan. The value of such a plan, the Division maintained,

. . .is that it sets out, for all to see, why the community is changing and how it will develop in the near future. Situations can be debated and problems resolved before they reach crisis proportions. Compromises can be worked out among conflicting interests before the parties involved are forced into fixed positions. Decisions can be made on the basis of tomorrow's needs, not just today's and yesterday's. People know what to expect and can take action accordingly; uncertainty and misunderstanding can be minimized.[39]

The proposed plan did set out, in general terms, the pattern of change facing the community, and it was adopted by Port Hawkesbury, which to a considerable extent lived within its confines. In doing so the town attempted to anticipate its needs and to minimize the social costs of expansion. Yet, as has been suggested, those social costs were still very high. As far as can be made out from the meagre statistics available, they were much higher than necessary. In the following pages the reasons why this was so will be examined.

The Province and Development Planning

Port Hawkesbury did not make the most of the opportunities presented by development at Point Tupper because it was not allowed to do so. Development meant that the town's efforts to provide its citizens with decent social amenities became unusually dependent on international economic conditions and decisions made in distant board rooms; on the policies of senior governments; and on the attitudes of neighbouring communities. Dependence is a condition of modern life, and communities far larger than Port Hawkesbury have had to accept stringent limitations on their ability to develop appropriate responses to changing social and economic conditions. Nevertheless, Port Hawkesbury's efforts to grapple with the consequences of Point Tupper's development were constrained to such an extent by external agencies - particularly by the actions of other governments - that the town's experience must give pause to any community that looks to development to alleviate economic difficulties.

Of these external agencies the provincial government was the most critical actor. International business decisions and world economic conditions created the framework for Port Hawkesbury's expansionary cycle, and that framework was delineated more sharply by federal government policies. But for the most part decisions taken at these levels had little to do with the day-to-day operations of the town. They determined whether or not Point Tupper would have more workers and Port Hawkesbury more citizens. They also determined what kind of work was performed at Point Tupper, thus defining the nature of the work force - skilled, unskilled or professional - and, to some extent, the level of services those workers would expect. Certain aspects of federal government policy - its DREE, Environment, and Manpower programs in particular - had greater immediacy, but even in these fields constitutional factors ensured that the federal authority would play a role essentially subordinate to and supportive of that of the province.* The latter, because of its constitutional responsibility for local government and its determination to spearhead the drive for industrial development, was in the best position to create a coordinated social and industrial development policy, integrating Canso's boom in a provincial master plan and providing a regional framework for the orderly assimilation of the changes at Point Tupper.

*The relative importance of the federal, provincial, and municipal governments in the Strait development process is assessed more fully in a later part of this study.

The Province did not do this. As one provincial Development Minister, the Hon. Ralph Fiske, later admitted, the social services and accompanying infrastructure in the region did not get the same measure of attention that industrial development received.[40] In fact, throughout the period of expansion at the Strait, the planning role of the provincial government was hard to determine. Local authorities, aware that Halifax "pretty well controls the strings", became increasingly concerned at the confusion created as each of a dozen provincial agencies applied policies that conflicted with one another and ignored local needs. Community leaders took to heart the Community Planning Division's warning that:

> At the local level, and particularly in the main growth centre of Port Hawkesbury, [planning] means 'instant planning' for almost immediate development. The pressures of growth require quick preparation for development. New problems are added to those already plaguing municipal government: inadequate staff, not enough finances, little experience with rapid growth, and no means for dealing with such difficult but basic municipal responsibilities as helping people find adequate housing. Careful planning, based on thorough study and analysis, is necessary to overcome these obstacles and build an orderly, efficient and attractive community.[41]

The Mayor and councillors soon concluded unhappily that the Province had no intention of following its own advice.

An early issue was the problem of the town's water supply. Much of the town was dependent on deep wells which frequently failed, and many had to have their water carted in. While Nova Scotia Pulp's need for a secure and plentiful water supply had been met, the town's repeated requests for assistance in providing a similar supply to its expanded population were answered only in the later 1960s.[42] Another source of conflict between the local area and the provincial government arose when town officials represented to the provincial government the need for greatly expanded school facilities. The Department of Education, according to Arthur J. Langley, Jr., who was mayor at the time, ridiculed suggestions that the town would need school facilities as large as it fancied. The town did get permission to build a 12-room school which was overcrowded on the day that it was opened. In the view of the local people, Department of Education officials lacked both foresight and willingness to consider the assessment of those with on-the-spot experience.[43] Resentment of Halifax's control and apparent lack of understanding, always present in the area, was intensified as delegation after delegation returned home empty-handed. Before Boom Two was far advanced, residents of Port Hawkesbury had added to these grievances a catalogue of decisions perpetrated by provincial agencies with little reference to one another or to the community.

A trunk access route to Point Tupper, built by the Department of

Highways, cut through a mobile home park designed by the Community Planning Division as a model of its kind. The location of the heavy water plant at Point Tupper made sense to development officials; with the thermal generating plant and the oil refinery, it could be the nucleus of a petrochemical industry. Unfortunately, medical authorities were not consulted. They have since pointed out that the plant's proximity is a hazard to Port Hawkesbury and makes the town a poor location for the much-needed regional hospital. In the unlikely event of a disastrous gas leakage or explosion, Port Hawkesbury would be too close to the danger area. Locating the plant even a short distance away from its present site would have obviated this problem.[44] Again, despite expansionist rhetoric, some departments seemed unaware of the implications of Point Tupper's expansion. The Department of Municipal Affairs resisted pleas to treat the region, and particularly Port Hawkesbury, as a special case. Yet, while the department was refusing to provide special growth assistance to the town, and so forcing it to assume an excessive debt, other provincial agencies were successfully persuading Ottawa that the region should be designated a special growth area. Eventually this led to a situation in which federal money was used to plan and promote projects that provincial agencies considered too ambitious or even unnecessary. This exacerbated tensions between province and town still further.

Elements within the provincial government recognized the problems of agency isolationism. "The large number of government bodies involved in the area", one internal review suggested, referring to all levels of government, "was a deterrent to achievement."[45] In general, however, provincial spokesmen have rejected this view. Ralph Fiske, speaking to a 1971 conference, maintained that provincial planning, in the formal sense at any rate, was initiated as early as April 1966, when sessions between government and industry developed the idea of an integrated industrial complex at Point Tupper. He went on:

> By the mid-1960's, it became obvious that increased planning and coordination were essential for the continuing and future development of the Strait area. The province commissioned several studies of the area, including the Henry J. Kaiser Canada Ltd. Master Plan of the site conditions in the area, with development guidelines for efficient use of the harbour. MacNamara Engineering prepared an overall plan for the industrial land in the area, and the province cooperated with and assisted Gulf Oil in preparing the Bechtel Report on Industrial Possibilities and Environmental Considerations in the Strait Area. In 1970 the provincially commissioned study of the feasibility of establishing a liquid and dry bulk deepwater redistribution terminal was released by the Department of Development.[46]

Although the need for planning and coordination may have been recognized "by the mid-1960's", results were achieved very slowly. In

October 1967 C.M. Drury, then Minister of Industry and of Defence Production, referred to the lack of planning activity in the region as follows:

> There is as yet no formulated plan for the development or exploitation of this advantage [the advantages of the deepwater harbour], but the whole question of the further development of Cape Breton, including a deepwater port at Port Hawkesbury, is now under urgent consideration by a committee of officials from the departments which have an interest in this matter.[47]

As Drury's comments suggested, even overall development strategy was protracted - and without such a strategy essential community planning encountered too many uncertainties to be productive. Delivery of a report on a Point Tupper Industrial Park Plan in May 1968 revealed, for example, that nine years after expropriation of land for the park the provincial government was still considering basic plans for the site.[48] Again it was not until 1968 that a Strait of Canso Coordinating Committee was set up to keep track of the wide range of activities by different divisions of the Nova Scotia government in relation to the activities of the federal government, private industry locating on the site, and the host of consulting engineering and planning organizations required.[49] In addition, a Strait of Canso Planning Commission was projected to help implement regional planning in the area. The Strait of Canso Coordinating Committee consisted of the Minister of Trade and Industry, Chairman, the Provincial Secretary, Mr. Gerald Doucet, who was then M.L.A. for the area, and also included civil servants. It was charged with coordinating interdepartmental activities in the industrial development area. As well, it was intended to provide liaison between industry and federal, provincial, and municipal governments. The Committee's influence, however, appears to have been limited. It is not referred to in the numerous reports on Strait development prepared by government during this period; few of the officials interviewed recalled its existence.

In October 1970, fourteen years after Stora Kopparberg identified the Strait's potential, the provincial Cabinet Committee on Planning and Programs received a consultant's report on economic strategy for the region.[50] The report underlined the need for a prompt and vigorous coordination of programs for the region:

> There will need to be a concerted effort if the present population is to maximize and consolidate its gains from the development and development potential of the area. There is potential for vigorous and relevant education and training programs to result in large numbers of the present population embarking on new and more secure vocations. There is also the possibility that, if the government and people of the area do not initiate change and respond to new opportunities, then large sections

of the existing population may be by-passed in the real gains in development. Reform of nearly all the existing social institutions in a coordinated and responsive manner is needed as soon as possible.51

The month the report was delivered a provincial general election brought about defeat of the incumbent government, the subsequent dismantling of the agency responsible for considering the report, the reorganization of the related agencies, and the reconsideration of all policy proposals. Among the report's other recommendations to be abandoned were the creation of an entirely new community to accommodate the expected increased population at a reasonable distance from the environmental and safety hazards of Point Tupper, and the suggestion that:

Development controls should be introduced, coordinated and enforced for the whole Strait area. Complementary with these development controls, a land acquisition program is proposed for the long term development of recreation in the area. This is designed to preserve intact, and unspoiled, areas for both present and future public recreation use.52

In November 1971, Allan J. MacEachen, then President of the Privy Council and Member of Parliament, Cape Breton Highlands-Canso, referred to the lack of planning during this period as follows:

I have been aware personally for some years that things weren't really going all that well in this area. Even when we were at the very peak of our construction boom. I was aware, and many of you were aware, that things weren't going all that well. But, because of the momentum of the atmosphere in which we lived from day to day, it was an experience we will all remember. I am also aware that the development which did take place and, hopefully, will continue to take place, happened largely by haphazard decisions and haphazard methods. Certainly, many of the major decisions which were made by government, industry and unions, were never very closely related to the people themselves. Or , to put it another way, I didn't find that the people - the residents of this area - very much influenced or very much controlled the decisions that shaped their lives, their environment and their future.53

Subsequent provincial policy, although representing a marginal improvement over that of the 1960s, has still not permitted Strait area residents to significantly influence, much less control, these decisions.

The Lang Reports: The Failure of Anticipatory Planning
Although development activity at the provincial level tended in general to be poorly planned and fragmented, one agency with a mandate to introduce province-wide planning saw the situation at the Strait as a challenge and an opportunity. This was the Department of Municipal

Affairs' Community Planning Division (CPD) which, as noted in the discussion of development in Bridgewater, exercises the provincial responsibility for initiating planning activity, providing the necessary technical support, giving final approval for plans and by-laws, and, in special circumstances, intervening in municipal planning administration.[54]

By 1968 the CPD was emerging as a force to be reckoned with in Nova Scotia municipal administration. For many years confined by the limited role prescribed for it by the Town Planning Act, the Division launched, in April 1968, a major review of the province's planning legislation.[55]

> Certain weaknesses in the existing Town Planning Act were apparent; despite periodic amendments, the Act still contained the basic framework devised in 1939. But more fundamental was the feeling that the Town Planning Act had simply not been effective, that many people talked favourably about planning but few municipal units possessed the determination and/or the capability to act on their general planning convictions. Comprehensive, larger-scale, more concerted efforts seemed necessary to cope with economic, social and environmental change as Nova Scotia moved into the Seventies.[56]

The review and the Planning Act of 1969 which resulted spelled out a more extensive and authoritative role for the Division, and the situation at the Strait offered an excellent opportunity to develop and test that new role. The urgent need for a scheme of orderly development in Port Hawkesbury would demonstrate the applicability of the Division's professional skills, while success in achieving some coordination on the part of the eight municipalities in the area would establish the Division's position as an integral part of municipal administration in the province.* Furthermore, the situation at the Strait presented a classic illustration of the need to integrate industrial and social development policy, and it became a major objective of the planning review and the Planning Act to bring about such an integration:

> Regional planning, while linking together municipal planning, will be closely tied into the province's development strategy. The effect of this two-way process will be that *all* our planning, and especially programming and implementation, will be more responsive to local, regional, and also to the provincial needs and opportunities.[57]

---

*Although the Community Planning Division gave high priority to planning developments at the Strait, the Department itself, according to Mayor Langley, was cool to Town requests for assistance in planning. Observers of the Department of Municipal Affairs during this period generally believe that the Department, through its then Deputy Minister, did not encourage planning activity and that members of the Community Planning Division had little influence over policy. The Planning Review was, consequently, not only an opportunity to revise an outdated piece of legislation, but an attempt to enhance the status of the Community Planning Division itself. Successful involvement with the events at Port Hawkesbury would contribute to this goal.

Effective integration of industrial and social development planning at the Strait would go far to secure for community planning in general a role in province-wide planning activity.

The obvious and urgent need, coupled with the opportunity to develop a more effective role at the department, local, regional, and even provincial levels, offered compelling incentives for the Community Planning Division's vigorous promotion of planning at the Strait. Other factors were also at work. In particular, some prospective tenants at Point Tupper were demonstrating an interest in local social conditions. The Gulf Oil Company, in conjunction with the Community Planning Division, commissioned the Bechtel Company to look into this aspect of its possible location at Point Tupper. In the Point Tupper site. They favoured establishing a refinery at Point Tupper, but pointed out the lack of adequate community facilities in the area and the need for planning. They noted that the water system was still inadequate for the needs of the industrial complex and for the community, pointing out that there were freshwater sources adequate to service these needs but that a development program was still required to bring water to the complex. The incapacity of the labour force to carry out the skilled construction assignments necessary to staff the industry itself was a further problem, as was the lack of suitable training facilities for local labour. A final report of October 1967 concluded that:

> Maximum benefits can only be obtained through controlled and orderly growth, and that growth on such a large scale will be accompanied by many problems. One of the more serious will be the requirements of adequate housing and facilities for the operating force and employees of the service industries supporting the complex. Although nearby communities will initially accommodate some of the new people coming into the area, entirely new communities will have to be developed.
> To provide new facilities in an orderly manner, plans and standards for both industrial and community development must be devised and adopted early in the program. Firm but realistic environmental standards are essential for the benefit of industry and residents of both the new community and the presently existing areas. If these plans and standards are adequate, individual plants can be arranged to complement other establishments, and other savings and investment and operating costs may be realized. At the same time, the residential and business communities can be made attractive. Orderly, planned expansion will thus be for the benefit of all.[58]

Local officials were also concerned that development in the area should be put on a more orderly footing. This sentiment was strongest in Port Hawkesbury where, "in the light of population projections suggested by federal and provincial industrial development officers, the town had begun a rapid and extensive expansion of public services." In 1968, for example, the town issued 20-year debentures for $1,150,000 to finance construction of schools, sewers, streets, and water facilities. A further $76,000 was borrowed from the province.[59] Although this was the first major borrowing undertaken by the town, it nevertheless represented a considerable burden for a community of approximately 2,000 people and a limited tax base. Furthermore, additional large-scale borrowings would have to be made in successive years. For those in Port Hawkesbury responsible for setting the tax rate the situation was distressingly clear: unless residential and small business development in the Strait area were carefully directed, the town would find itself struggling to provide essential services for the region while business and much residential construction would avoid the consequent high taxes by locating outside the town limits. Port Hawkesbury's financial viability depended on a regional plan that recognized and sustained the town's role as the regional centre.

With interest in community planning building at the local level, among potential investors, and within the responsible government agency, it was not long before concrete steps were taken. A period of intense planning activity began in 1966,[60] which led, in December 1967, to the issuing of a Strait of Canso Regional Development Plan Proposal and, several months later, to a Proposed Development Plan for the Town of Port Hawkesbury, a plan which was designed to dovetail with the larger regional plans. Both plans were primarily the work of the then head of the Community Planning Division, Reg Lang. The thrust of these reports, which are known as the *Lang Reports,* was that development should be quite closely controlled in the immediate region of Port Hawkesbury with a view to creating in the town a sufficient assessment base to provide services required by the town itself and the expanded population of the region. Regional and local development at the Strait were to go "hand in hand", and most of the new development, "at least until 1970 or thereabouts", was to be channelled into Port Hawkesbury.[61]

In Port Hawkesbury itself the proposed town plan suggested an orderly opening of development opportunities, with much of the townsite closed to expansion until existing residential and business areas had been occupied. In this fashion the costs of providing serviced lands would not run ahead of the rate of development. In a general sense, the town has observed these provisions, which were incorporated in the necessary zoning by-law some months after the presentation of the proposed plan for the town (February 1968). At this time the town was engaged in a three-year improvement program which included upgrading and paving of existing streets, installation of sanitary and storm sewers, and construction of a sewage treatment plant. Its problems with water still continued, but consulting engineers had been engaged to inquire further into the problem and to look into the possibility of hooking up the town's supply system with the industrial water supply system developed for Point Tupper.[62] The plan encouraged the continuation of such improvements but recognized the financial burden they represented. In dealing with the capital budget, the plan pointed out that:

> Port Hawkesbury's financial difficulties so far have been dealt with by the Town and the Department of Municipal Affairs on an ad hoc basis. The prospect of further growth, and facilities, both for itself and the Region, make it imperative that a long-term financial solution be found.
> The Regional Development Plan recommends that a five year fiscal plan be prepared for the Region. This would establish priorities for and estimate costs of community facilities and services, and assign responsibility for providing them. The fiscal plan would include both Municipal and Provincial expenditures in the region. The Town's capital budget would form a cornerstone of the regional budget 63

Lang's proposals for regional coordination, however, proved unacceptable to all the municipalities except Port Hawkesbury. Richmond County, for example, agreed that industrial zoning should take place, but objected to the suggestion that all secondary industry should be located in Port Hawkesbury.64 Richmond would agree to tax sharing and fuller cooperation, but not to the degree of integration envisaged by Lang. In general, it was felt that although the reports might be technically excellent they focused too heavily on Port Hawkesbury and did not reflect the thinking of the other councils involved. These resisted implementation of the regional plan, and in 1969 the province, accepting their view, sought another approach to regional coordination.

Reviews, Commissions, and Political Uncertainty
The development of planning proposals by the CPD was not entirely fruitless. It had served to bring municipal officials into more frequent contact with one another and to break down some mutual distrust. Although Lang's proposals were rejected, discussions continued. Influenced, in the view of one observer, by fear of provincial intervention, eventually "the six municipal units bordering the Strait expressed to the Minister of Municipal Affairs their interest in becoming directly involved in a review of local government in their area."65 A lengthy reassessment of the situation at the Strait began in September 1969. An elaborate structure for tackling the impact of development throughout the Strait area was developed. Representing the eight municipalities at the Strait, the review's Steering Committee was composed of the mayors or wardens of the municipalities, their deputies, and the clerk-treasurers. The Province was represented by the Minister of Municipal Affairs and his Deputy Minister, while local MLA's were invited to join the committee on an *ex officio* basis. A part-time secretary, W.F. McKee, was seconded to the committee from the Cape Breton Development Corporation and given staff support by the Department of Municipal Affairs and the provincial

Secretariat for Planning and Programs. Field work was carried out by a group of five resource development representatives from the Nova Scotia Department of Agriculture and Marketing. The committee was charged with studying the organization and administration of local government structures, analyzing future demands, and considering alternative forms of government.

The committee, in its own words, proceeded slowly, "deliberately so in order that its members would have sufficient opportunity to become fully informed on the many complex issues."[66] Not being a decision-making body, the committee attempted to operate on a consensus basis with a view to presenting the participating councils with recommendations that all members of the committee could endorse. Commissioning T.J. Plunkett Associates of Montreal to study "the basis for amalgamation or consolidation as a separate consideration for each side of the Strait", the committee delivered its report in May 1971. This document noted "that the present structure of municipal government doesn't allow councils and their staff to handle effectively the many demands placed on them, and that this situation will get worse - as growth continues at the Strait."[67] Its major recommendation was the consolidation of the eight municipal units into two, one on each side of the Strait.

Once again, however, the planning effort was aborted. By 1971 the Royal Commission on Education, Public Services and Provincial Municipal Relations (the Graham Commission) had been appointed by the Nova Scotia Government, and it was clear that its final recommendations would materially affect not only the structure of local government at the Strait but also the entire framework within which Nova Scotia municipalities had operated for decades. At the urging of provincial officials and of the Commission itself the proposals of the *Local Government Review,* like so many earlier recommendations, were held in abeyance pending delivery of the *Graham Report* and consideration of its recommendations by the province.

In the meantime, to sustain the level of intermunicipal cooperation achieved by the *Local Government Review,* the Steering Committee was reconstituted to include representatives of local Planning Advisory Committees and undertook detailed examinations of planning needs in the region. Task groups were assigned to study land use, environmental factors, socio-economic problems, and so on. In the view of one observer, these came to be dominated by federal and provincial civil servants who "belatedly decided to get involved in whatever was happening there."[68] Loose terms of reference, lack of specific deadlines, and a somewhat abstract approach to the region's needs rendered their work less and less valuable in the eyes of the local community.

Waiting for the Graham Commission's report was a mistake.

Although the town derived some comfort from the sympathetic stance of the report, its controversial general recommendations entailed a long debate at the provincial level, and its proposed reorganization of the Strait region into one community, rather than the two suggested by the local government review, [69] aroused local antagonism. The report's appearance signalled the beginning of another round of discussion and delay.

The period between the rejection of Lang's proposals in 1969 and delivery of the Graham report in 1974 was, however, not completely disappointing. The Lang exercises and the local government review, together with the experience of living through Boom Two, seem to have rubbed away a good deal of the parochialism that is said to have separated the Strait communities. Much still divides them, but one has the impression that a long-standing preoccupation with local rights and perquisites is slowly giving way to a regional approach to community affairs.

A considerably more tangible development occurred when in 1969 the Government of Nova Scotia and the Government of Canada agreed that the Strait of Canso should be designated a Special Incentives Area under the federal government's regional assistance program. The designation brought three major benefits as far as Port Hawkesbury was concerned. First, the town became eligible for various grants and loans from the federal government, including grants and loans in support of infrastructure development. Second, as a result of this support Port Hawkesbury successfully applied for assistance in developing plans for a major school and community centre. A further $1,000,000 loan and matching grant was promised towards construction of the complex. The agreement also meant that federal involvement in planning for industrial development was extended to general regional and community planning. [70]

The second and last of these benefits deserve additional comment. The school-community centre feasibility study - Project 3.9, as it is called locally - generated far more than an excellent proposal for a combined facility. By using an elaborate mix of participative techniques the consultants, Graham, Napier, Hébert and Associates, succeeded not only in achieving a high level of involvement in the project, they focused community interest on the planning process itself, fostering support for planning and creating a climate receptive to further extensions of citizen participation. The techniques employed included interviews with community leaders and officials and sessions with group representatives and citizens at large, as well as surveys and the operation of a drop-in centre for those interested in the development of the study. But the heart of the technique was the application of a critical path approach to citizen participation, which, by carefully marking each step of the planning process and encouraging full participation at each step, created a sense of achievement as well as of involvement. That is, the interested members of the community not only had a sense of participating in the project, but they could see, as each stage was reached, how far they had come and how far there was yet to go. The sense of aimlessness that frequently undermines citizen participation in community development projects was consequently reduced.

The effects of this exercise are still reverberating in the community. The momentum built up in support of the complex has carried over into negotiations between the Province and the town concerning its realization. Provincial agencies have been reluctant to endorse the project and, at the time of writing, have delayed making a decision. Strong local support for the project has assisted the efforts of municipal politicians who wished to impress provincial authorities with the need for the program. Among other products of the 3.9 exercise has been an apparent heightened sense of community, a clarification of needs and objectives, and a growth in awareness of the possibilities of citizen participation, an awareness that played a part in the Port Hawkesbury municipal election of 1973 and saw a new mayor greatly extend the opportunities for citizen involvement in council and subcommittees.[71]

Apart from Project 3.9, the extension of DREE's participation in community and regional planning, made possible by the 1969 agreement, has not been easy to identify. Federal participation in Steering Committee task forces has been noted; it has also been noted that this seems not to have been significant. DREE has maintained no office in the Strait region, and has not been permitted by the province to take an active, continuing part in planning for the region.[72] Perhaps the most significant aspect of federal involvement is contained in the 1975 renewal of the federal-provincial agreement. The Strait of Canso subsidiary agreement, as well as providing for continued infrastructure support, requires the establishment of a Strait of Canso Development Office to "take the leadership role in development at the Strait of Canso", to report to the Minister of Development, and to be headed by "a highly qualified person with proven success and experience in both public and private sectors." The office will have a staff of fifteen to twenty-five. Its functions are described as:

(a) Planning: to be responsible for development planning for the Strait of Canso Region, and to coordinate municipal and social planning for the Strait of Canso in cooperation with the Strait of Canso Steering Committee, to ensure that it meshes with industrial development plans.

(b) Coordination: to cooperate with the Strait of Canso Steering Committee in coordinating municipal and provincial government activities at the Strait of Canso in terms of services, regulatory policy, etc., and to work with the federal government to ensure that federal government activities are consistent with those of the municipalities and the Province.

(c) Management:

  1. to promote and develop industrial activity through the identification of opportunities and to investigate any and all methods of capitalizing upon these opportunities;

  2. to conduct negotiations with public and private interests to bring to a successful conclusion the opportunities which have been identified;

  3. to administer all provincially-owned industrial land in the Strait of Canso;

  4. to stimulate and facilitate the development of all necessary commercial, recreational, and community infrastructure and amenities commensurate with the pace of overall development activity; and

  5. to be responsible for the coordination of the development of all provincially-owned industrial, transportation and communications infrastructure within the region.[73]

Presumably, if the office is not operational and demonstrating a capacity to meet these objectives by 1977, when the present agreement expires, federal involvement in the Strait region will be curtailed. A concomitant feature of the subsidiary agreement is financial support for integrated regional community and development planning.

In addition to Project 3.9 and other aspects of federal involvement at the Strait, the Province, in 1973, made a move that has important implications for development planning in the Canso region. This was the appointment of a regional development coordinator for the Strait area, Alex Harris. One of the most significant developments in the recent history of the Strait, Harris' appointment provides a point of field liaison between the various federal and provincial agencies operating there. He is an obvious contact point between these agencies and local governments and, despite the fact that he is an employee of the Department of Development, has been able to facilitate relations between the municipalities and the various agency headquarters in Halifax and Ottawa.* For the provincial leadership, he has provided an important overview of local needs and feelings. His office serves as a base for employees of the Community Planning Division and Department of the Environment engaged in developing the regional plan and in carrying out an assessment of the environmental effects of proposed further industrial development at

---

*His functions are officially described as "to serve as the senior government representative in the area and provide the local coordination point in the maximization of government development. His duties also include coordinative of all aspects of development at the Strait, including economic development, industrial planning and regional planning. As well, the Coordinator serves as the Executive Officer, Strait of Canso Steering Committee, and supported in all aspects of its activity." *Terms of Reference for Port Hastings - Port Hawkesbury - Point Tupper Development Plan* (draft, April 22, 1974, mimeo.), pp. 9-10.

Point Tupper and Mulgrave. With his encouragement, the Steering Committee's planning task forces, referred to above, have been remodelled along the lines that had proved so successful in Project 3.9. They now include a large number of citizens from the region and consider issues that are clearly defined and of immediate and obvious importance.[74]

The Price of Delay
While the Community Planning Division developed and the region discussed and eventually rejected the Lang proposals, the social problems referred to earlier became increasingly serious. As the local government review and the Graham Commission deliberated, these problems were excerbated by delay and by the mounting pressure created by the construction boom. Port Hawkesbury's very compliance with the well-intentioned advice of the Community Planning Division has compounded the difficulties it has had to face.

The Division's proposals depended for their success on the implementation of a regional plan. Although Port Hawkesbury accepted the plan prepared for it by Reg Lang, the fact that neither Richmond nor Inverness Counties had accepted the proposed regional plan meant that the town's scheme was jeopardized. The full meaning of this became clear when the town acted upon the Division's recommendation that it install public utilities designed to accommodate a considerably larger anticipated population, rather than the one then living in Port Hawkesbury. As a later Town Council pointed out:

> To the extent that provincial and federal programs to stimulate economic growth in the Strait of Canso area are successful, the Town of Port Hawkesbury must continue to plan for a growing population with growing needs for municipal services. The rate of growth is difficult to predict, but it is imperative that services be available when they are required . . . . The implications of such forward planning are that expenditures have to be made before the taxpayers who will use the services have taken up residence in the Town.[75]

The town invested in water services and public utilities capable of serving a far larger community, and did what it could to meet a sudden large increase in demand for educational and other social services.

When it came to financing these expenditures, however, officials in the Grants and Finances Division of the Department of Municipal Affairs, who were responsible for vetting most aspects of municipal budgeting in the province, reacted quite differently from their colleagues in the Community Planning Division. Unimpressed with the view that the town had to plan for unprecedented future growth, they argued that Port Hawkesbury was "living beyond its means". Suggestions that special assistance grants were needed to meet the "explosive" growth situation at the Strait were met with the response that the Province could not do for Port Hawkesbury what it would not do for other communities in Nova Scotia. It could not set a precedent. Eventually the Province did conclude that these installations could be financed through a succession of debenture issues on which the province granted a five-year deferral of payment of principal and interest (see Table 7 and Figure 4).

Had the CPD's proposed regional development plan been implemented, this position might not have been unreasonable. By concentrating population and small businesses in and near to Port Hawkesbury, the CPD plan would have promoted optimal use of public services and provided an assessment base capable of supporting them. The CPD plan was not implemented, however, and Port Hawkesbury soon found that its taxes were considerably out of line with those in neighbouring municipalities. As the Graham Commission pointed out*, the 1972 average per capita tax in Port Hawkesbury was three and a half times that in Richmond County:

Town of Port Hawkesbury	$ 78.88
Town of Mulgrave	43.54
Municipality of the County of Inverness	31.54
Municipality of the County of Antigonish	29.54
Municipality of the County of Richmond	22.44
Municipality of the County of Guysborough	20.59
Town of Canso	20.00[76]

By 1973 the town, which by now had a population of between 3,400 and 3,600 and an assessment roll valued at $19,143,850, had a debt load of $6,700,000. In 1972 gross debt charges represented 34.9 per cent of estimated revenue.[77] Under Nova Scotia's market value assessment scheme, many homeowners found themselves paying real property taxes of $1,000 or more on a tax rate of $2.70 that was expected to rise to $5.54 in 1975 and perhaps to $8.29 by 1977. Compared to other communities, Port Hawkesbury's average per household tax was one of the highest in the province (see Table 8).

Faced with the prospect of paying Port Hawkesbury's extremely high taxes, newcomers, business and individuals, have settled in "the

---

*The Commission also pointed out that Port Hawkesbury's position, along with that of other communities, was weakened by the practice of industrial properties receiving a "tax holiday".

"The federal government grants are close to the equivalent of actual taxation, but the provincial grants are much more arbitrary and usually fall far short of normal taxes . . . . the municipalities around the Strait of Canso are steadily and dramatically losing control of their own tax base." (Graham Report, II.5-288.)

These sums are distributed according to a formula which sees Port Hawkesbury receive 32 per cent of the grants for the Point Tupper facilities other than that for Nova Scotia Forest Industries, which reflects the distribution of the company's timber lands as well as its employees.

Figure 4

PORT HAWKESBURY: DEBT ACCUMULATION, 1961-1973
SHOWING EXPENDITURE CATEGORIES

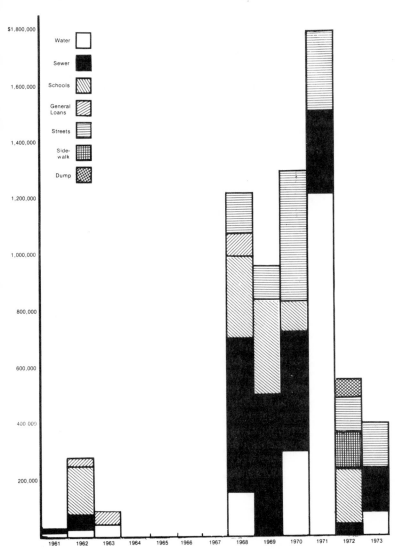

Source: Town of Port Hawkesbury, *Financial Problems of the Town of Port Hawkesbury, Submission to the Department of Municipal Affairs, February 26th, 1974,* Appendix 18, pp. 26-28.

Table 7

SCHEDULE OF PRINCIPAL OUTSTANDING, DEBENTURE ISSUES AND LOANS, TOWN OF PORT HAWKESBURY, 1973 [WITH PROJECTIONS FOR 1974-77]

1) WATER:

- $ 12,000 issued in 1961 for 20 years at 5 3/4%.
- $ 33,000 issued in 1962 for 20 years at 5 3/4%.
- $ 55,000 issued in 1963 for 20 years at 5 3/4%.
*- $ 40,000 issues in 1968 for 20 years at 8%.
*- $122,000 issued in 1968 for 20 years at 8 1/2%.
*- $315,000 issued in 1970 for 20 years at 9 1/2%.
*- $490,000 issued in 1971 for 20 years at 9 3/4%.
*- $300,000 issued in 1971 for 20 years at 10%.
*- $434,000 issued in 1971 for 20 years at 8 3/4%.
*- $ 38,000 issued in 1971 for 20 years at 8 3/4%.
- $ 46,000 issued in 1973 for 20 years at 8 1/4%.
- $50,000 issued in 1973 for 20 years at 8 1/2%.

2) SEWER:

- $ 12,000 issued in 1961 for 20 years at 5 3/4%.
- $ 43,000 issued in 1962 for 20 years at 5 3/4%.
*- $100,000 issued in 1968 for 20 years at 8%.
*- $438,000 issued in 1968 for 20 years at 8 1/2%.
*- $500,000 issued in 1969 for 20 years at 9 1/2%.
*- $400,000 issued in 1970 for 20 years at 10%.
*- $ 12,000 issued in 1970 for 20 years at 9 3/4%.
.*- $ 64,000 issued in 1971 for 20 years at 8 3/4%.
*- $204,000 issued in 1971 for 20 years at 8 3/4%.
- $ 27,000 issued in 1972 for 20 years at 8 1/4%.
- $ 45,000 issued in 1973 for 20 years at 8 1/4%.
- $140,000 issued in 1973 for 20 years at 8 1/2%.

3) STREETS:

- $150,000 issued in 1968 for 20 years at 8%.
- $125,000 issued in 1969 for 20 years at 9 1/2%.
- $217,000 issued in 1970 for 20 years at 9 1/2%.
- $245,000 issued in 1970 for 20 years at 9 1/2%.
- $ 42,000 issued in 1971 for 20 years at 8 1/2%.
- $250,000 issued in 1971 for 20 years at 8 1/2%.
- $129,500 issued in 1972 for 20 years at 8 1/4%.
- $174,000 issued in 1973 for 20 years at 8 1/4%.

4) SIDEWALK:

- $129,500 issued in 1972 for 20 years at 8 1/4%.

5) DUMP:

- $ 57,000 issued in 1972 for 20 years at 8 1/4%.

6) STREET CONSTRUCTION, STREET LIGHTING, WATER AND SEWAGE LINES

- 1975, Issue of $800,000 for 20 years at 9% to finance projected increases a improvements to water, sewer, street and sidewalk facilities (see paragra 12 of "Financial Problems of the Town of Port Hawkesbury").
- 1976, Issue of $800,000 for 20 years at 9% to finance projected increa and improvements to water, sewer, street and sidewalk facilities (see pa graph 12 of "Financial Problems. . .").
- 1977, Issue of $800,000 for 20 years at 9% to finance projected increases a improvements to water, sewer, street and sidewalk facilities (see paragra 12 of "Financial Problems. . .").

7) SCHOOLS:

- $165,000 issued in 1962 for 20 years at 5 1/4%.
- $ 14,000 issued in 1962 for 20 years at 5 1/4%.
*- $300,000 issued in 1968 for 20 years at 8%.
*- $340,000 issued in 1969 for 20 years at 8 1/2%.
*- $110,000 issued in 1970 for 20 years at 9 1/2%.
*- $210,000 issued in 1972 for 20 years at 8 1/2%.

- 1975, Issue of $4,176,000 for 20 years at 9% to finance capital costs of Project 3.9 complex. (See Appendix 7, Scedule 4).
- 1975, Loan from DREE $1,000,000 for 20 years at 8% to finance capital costs of Project 3.9 complex. (See Appendix 7, Schedule 4).

8) LOANS - Province of Nova Scotia:
- $ 30,000 issued in 1962 for 5 years at 5 3/4%.
- $ 40,000 issued in 1963 for 5 years at 5 3/4%.
- $ 76,000 issued in 1968 for 10 years at 8 3/4%.

9) HOSPITAL:
- 1975, Issue of $1,200,000 for 20 years at 9% to finance capital cost of hospital. (See: *Town of Port Hawkesbury Five Year Budget Projection*, 1973-77, Schedule 2, Grants and Finance Division, Department of Municipal Affairs).

* Debenture issues on which Province of Nova Scotia has granted a five year deferral on payment of principal and interest.

Source: Town of Port Hawkesbury, *Financial Problems of Town of Port Hawkesbury*, Submission to the Department of Municipal Affairs, February 26th, 1974, Appendix 18, pp. 26-28.

Table 8

DEBT LOAD, TOWNS WITH POPULATION 2,500-5,500
NOVA SCOTIA, 1972

Town	Population (2,500 - 5,500)	Total net debt charges as a percentage of gross estimated revenue	Gross debt charges as a percentage of gross estimated revenue	Taxes as a percentage of gross estimated revenue	Avera per house tax $
Antigonish	5489	19.1	21.5	76.4	386.
Digby	2363	11.4	11.4	58.9	206.
Dominion	2879	9.4	10.2	30.4	164.
Kentville	5198	12.5	15.4	77.1	317.
Liverpool	3654	4.8	6.6	58.8	208.
Louisbourg	1582	32.1	32.1	52.3	175.
Lunenburg	3215	2.9	4.2	79.4	344.
Middleton	1870	13.8	18.8	66.3	284.
Parrsboro	1807	17.1	17.1	54.4	175.
Pictou	4250	8.7	12.4	46.8	188.
Port Hawkesbury	3372	33.6	34.9	60.3	310.
Shelburne	2689	13.6	14.7	50.9	197.
Springhill	6262	12.1	13.3	35.7	174.
Stellarton	5357	8.7	9.2	57.3	219.
Trenton	3331	14.6	15.1	86.7	228.
Westville	3898	30.9	38.5	43.9	126.
Windsor	3775	15.1	15.1	74.6	323.
Wolfville	2861	7.3	18.5	73.1	319.

Source: Town of Port Hawkesbury, *Financial Problems of the Town of Port Hawkesbury,* Submission to the Department of Municipal Affairs, February 26th, 1974, Appendix 1, p. 9.

rural hinterlands in ribbon development."[78] They have continued to look to the town, however, to supply regional services, and the town has continued to feel obliged to meet their demands. By 1974, anticipating the building of the school and community centre complex and participating in the construction of a regional hospital, town officials were convinced that their troubles had only begun:

> The problem of meeting debt charges for past capital works pales in comparison to the dilemma facing Town Council in attempting to meet and anticipate the needs of the continued growth implicit in the projected industrialization programs carried forward by the province in concert with the federal authorities. The Town cannot possibly be expected to carry the burdens imposed upon it by these developments since the present cost-sharing formula between the province and municipal units is not designed to cope with the type of explosive growth for which the Town of Port Hawkesbury is being asked to provide.[79]

Suggesting the development of a long-term formula for provincial assistance related to growth rate, in February 1974 the Council requested that, as an interim measure, the Province permit a further 5-year deferral of payments on Port Hawkesbury's 1967-68 agreements; provide a special growth grant to cover the entire capital costs of the school-community centre complex; contribute to other services; and assume the entire cost of construction of the proposed hospital.

By late 1974 the provincial government had responded to the town's appeal by providing a special grant of $278,000 to defray extraordinary debt charges. It had not indicated whether it would shift from its policy of treating Port Hawkesbury as a town like any other. No final decision had been made concerning the school-community centre complex and the hospital, although the Canada-Nova Scotia subsidiary agreement for 1975 provides $3.4 million for the project.* The town was left to draw what comfort it could from the fact that yet another external agent - this time world-wide recession - had cooled the drive for development and so given Port Hawkesbury time to adjust to the changes of the last decade and to continue to negotiate for essential services.

*At the time of publication (November 1975), the community centre portion of the complex had been funded under the Special Areas Agreement, with 75 per cent of the costs covered by an outright grant, and 25 per cent by a long term loan. Construction is under way, with an expected completion date of September, 1976.

A special provincially appointed commission recommended a Richmond County site for a new regional hospital in the early part of 1975. The proposed location met with strong opposition both from the County residents and from the Town of Port Hawkesbury. Subsequently, the Province announced that two separate but smaller hospitals would be built, one in the Louisdale area of Richmond County, and the second in Port Hawkesbury. Both new hospitals were formally approved by the Health Services and Insurance Commission in April of 1975, although construction tenders have not yet been called. The compromise solution has not stopped the vigorous public discussion surrounding the hospital needs of the area.

Development Planning and Failure at the Centre

Port Hawkesbury's is a story of opportunity lost, and ambition's unsatisfying achievement. Twenty years ago, the town looked to development as the guarantor of economic stability. Today, after a period of spectacular growth, uncertainty still dogs the town, and its future depends on vast organizations to whom it and its people mean virtually nothing. For many, development brought affluence. For others it brought disappointment. They lacked the skills or the union affiliation to obtain jobs at the construction sites, and the permanent positions created by the massive capital investment frequently went to itinerant professionals.[80] The original townspeople were on the periphery. Their few business leaders found themselves competing with and outbid by rivals from Sydney, Halifax, and larger centres. Their civic leaders were overwhelmed by the sophisticated bureaucracies of senior governments and saw their control over local events dwindle and disappear.[81] They took the "spin-off" jobs - the service jobs. They were paid more than in the past, but then inflation in a boom town destroyed their purchasing power, and for many municipal taxes became intolerably high. The services those taxes bought represented an improvement over what had existed in 1951. But most - water supplies, sewage, school expansion, paved roads - were the essential consequences of population explosion. Only to a limited degree - as in the provision of vocational training - have they meant a greater variety of opportunity. In fact, for those who lived in Port Hawkesbury in 1951, it is doubtful whether industrial development has improved the quality of life.

The central theme of this discussion of Port Hawkesbury's experience has been the striking lack of influence exercised by the people of the Strait area over the development taking place in their midst and over the measures adopted to adjust to expansion. When one considers the scale of investment industry has made at Point Tupper one can hardly be surprised that critical decisions depend on international economic conditions rather than the needs of local communities. A visitor to Port Hawkesbury finds this aspect of the local condition impressed upon him daily. He soon becomes intensely conscious of the news media. News reports are followed anxiously; any day may bring accounts of decisions in Halifax, Ottawa, New York, or London that will spell yet another cycle in the hectic life of this new-old town. The town itself can only wait, react, and hope.

But day to day control of events at Port Hawkesbury is exercised by the provincial government, not by the multinationals. The provincial government has been the agency that has assumed the responsibility for identifying and marketing the potential of the Strait of Canso. The province - with the federal government - has been responsible for developing manpower policies for the region. The province has traditionally exercised a paternalistic control over its creations, the municipalities. It has been responsible for ensuring that community development plans have been prepared and implemented, and for overseeing the financial state of the municipalities. If any level of government is to shoulder the major share of responsibility for the situation at the Strait, it must be the Province.

Specific agencies have performed well. Development officials brought to the region a spectacular industrial expansion. Community Planning officials worked hard to assist the region to plan for change. The Nova Scotia Housing Commission has helped to provide badly needed low-cost housing. Furthermore, it would be unreasonable to hold government entirely responsible for Port Hawkesbury's many disappointments. Even under the best of circumstances it is unlikely that the heady expectations of the late 1950s and early 1960s could have been realized, given the nature of the investment involved, its demand for skilled and professional labour, and the novelty of the situation. But the provincial government must share a good proportion of the blame for the failure of the Strait region to make the most of its period of expansion. The chief problems seem to have been an unnecessary rigidity in provincial attitudes to the situation at the Strait; poor communication between agencies; inadequate co-ordination; and lack of a general direction from the top.

Provincial rigidity is seen particularly in the unwillingness of Municipal Affairs officials to treat Port Hawkesbury's financial problems as a special case. But it is also present in the underlying attitude of the provincial government to the whole question of development at the Strait. Throughout the boom years the provincial government was preoccupied with attracting industry to the Strait. It seemed unable to adjust to the idea that once the potential of the deepwater harbour had been recognized, the business of marketing the Strait as an industrial location would become less important than the process of helping the Strait-side communities adjust to a revolution in their way of life. Only one provincial agency appears to have appreciated this point, and the CPD found itself unable to bring other elements of the provincial bureaucracy to share its views. The effects are observable in an unhappy school situation and an intolerable debt load for the Town of Port Hawkesbury.

Instances of poor communication between provincial agencies have been noted in the tendency of different agencies to follow policies incompatible with one another and sometimes harmful for the community. There was, for example, a failure on the part of development officials to appreciate the impact of their activities on the community, and consequently a failure to help planners and local officials anticipate developments. Some agencies have grossly underestimated the effects of development. A freer flow of information between agencies might have alerted organizations such as the

Department of Education and the Grants and Finance Division of the Department of Municipal Affairs to the need for a radical change of approach at the Strait.

Part and parcel with problems in communication was the lack of interagency co-ordination and general direction from the top. Particular attention will be paid to these aspects of the problem in the next chapter, but it is useful here to document their existence by referring to the same elements of policy confusion that are symptomatic of poor communications.

Provincial officials are apt to suggest that the intransigence of eight petty municipalities was the single greatest stumbling block to orderly development. The municipalities themselves recognized this problem. In the local government review, they wrote:

> We are unable to plan for or control development effectively. None of the units is large enough to employ the kinds of staff we need - for example, a group of engineers and planners. And no one of them, acting independently, is able to take advantage of economies of scale in the delivery of services.[82]

At every stage of community development, local animosities have been allowed to interfere with the well-intentioned proposals of federal and provincial officials and independent consultants. Lang's proposals were rejected. Richmond and Inverness Counties refused to control development in the vicinity of Port Hawkesbury, and their antagonism to the town doubtless influenced Halifax's attitude, making Strait planning "one of those issues hyper-sensitive to political paralysis."[83] "Why should Port Hawkesbury receive special treatment?" has been a constant complaint, and the town's investment in essential services is seen as an indulgence. Today the counties view the proposed school-community centre as unnecessarily luxurious, refusing to acknowledge the needs of an urban and relatively sophisticated population struggling to create a community where facilities are limited or nonexistent. Again, their views have influenced those of Halifax, affecting the level of financial assistance available to town and region and influencing the division of revenue between the municipalities. Most recently, local antagonisms have played their part in delaying plans to build a hospital in the Port Hawkesbury area. At issue - for safety reasons as well as local rivalries - is the location of the facility.[84]

Local jealousies have undoubtedly hindered the implementation of schemes that would have helped the residents of the region achieve an enviable standard of living and a desirable quality of life at reasonable cost. But the essential fact of local government in Nova Scotia is that the provincial government "controls the strings". It can, and occasionally does, completely reverse the decisions of municipal officials. Such a situation is open to abuse, and in Port Hawkesbury just as in Bridgewater, it has been possible for local power centres to achieve, through provincial intervention, objectives that might not have been won through the normal processes of local government decisions making. So, for example, the Province's decision not to build a bypass around Port Hawkesbury is attributed by some provincial officials not to short-sightedness on the part of the Department of Highways, but to the influence of local power centres who did not want through traffic diverted from the Reeves Street area.[85] Such interventions create the illusion of local influence while in effect undermining the authority of properly constituted municipal government.

Nowhere is the power of the provincial government more evident than in the role it plays in resolving intermunicipal disputes. It can, if it wishes, induce or coerce recalcitrant municipalities to follow desired courses of action. Yet at the Strait it is in this field that the lack of a firm provincial policy has created the most damage. By encouraging one municipality to adopt growth-oriented policies while permitting neighbouring communities to reject regional planning, the province has created a situation in which one municipality shoulders an intolerable debt load and its neighbours expose themselves to the worst effects of haphazard expansion. Again, in fostering an illusion of local influence, provincial failure to exercise leadership has created a situation in which genuine options for local initiative are progressively foreshortened.

Finally, the outsider can only be dismayed by the paucity of the resources available to Port Hawkesbury in its negotiations with these powerful outside agencies. Throughout the boom years, the town's administrative staff consisted of a town clerk, supported by two assistants, and a town engineer who had similar staff. No one in the town office possessed the necessary expertise to meet company and senior government officials on their own ground. No provincial agency seems to have tried to make up this deficiency by seconding competent staff to the town; consequently, a succession of town councils lacked a qualified internal source of advice and information concerning the many issues facing the community.

Port Hawkesbury's difficulties, however, stem less from internal weaknesses than from those we have identified at the provincial level. And at that level, too, the failure to achieve a multidimensional development policy goes further than a simple lack of communication between provincial agencies. Fragmentation of policy, interagency barriers, and timidity in the face of fractious local governments are very largely attributable to weakness at the political and administrative centre, a weakness to be explored at greater length in the following pages.

IV. THE PROVINCIAL APPROACH
   TO DEVELOPMENT

The Keystone of Development Policy

The dependence of local development planning on decision making at the provincial level has been stressed. In the case of Port Hawkesbury the major development problems encountered by the town must be attributed to weaknesses in the provincial policy system. Bridgewater was much less troubled by these weaknesses and, in fact, because of an ability to assimilate expansion and because of the nature of its development investment, relatively free of interference. Various difficulties between the town and the province were noted, however, which in a less richly endowed community, such as Port Hawkesbury, would have created very serious problems. The role of the province must now be examined more closely, considering first whether the provincial government really should be considered the key actor in Nova Scotia's industrial development experience and then attempting to understand why industrial and community development policy has failed to produce happier results in Port Hawkesbury and, to some extent, in Bridgewater.

In view of the previous discussion, there is no need to elaborate the assertion that local governments are virtually powerless to control industrial development affecting them; that power lies with industry and senior governments. Similarly, their real capacity to determine the nature of community development is very limited. Effective power lies at the provincial or federal level.

The role of the federal government is strikingly different from that of the municipalities. As the senior level of government, possessing vast financial and human resources, it is frequently supposed to exercise a dominating influence in the Atlantic region. It is not uncommon to hear Atlantic Canada referred to as Ottawa's "colony", and failures in regional planning and development are often attributed to the federal government's insistence on imposing central Canadian preconceptions on the solution of local problems.*

*- Senior civil servants in New Brunswick, for example, criticize federal attitudes towards plans for the province's Northeastern Region, stating that provincial plans were in effect ignored by federal officials who preferred to apply a traditional pork barrel approach (Confidential interview). Others, like James McGrath (*Chronicle-Herald*,

Undoubtedly Ottawa is influential. Its contributions to the Province's coffers ensure that. In 1960, for example, of Nova Scotia's $92 million net general revenue, the Government of Canada contributed $32 million in tax rental and equalization payments and $10 million in various other payments.[1] In 1970-71, equalization payments amounted to $93 million; income and estate taxes to $69.5 million; and other payments to $4 million.[2] As well, Ottawa contributes directly to numerous shared-cost schemes and incentives programs. In the four-year period, 1969-70 to 1972-73, its support of development planning and administration, industrial incentives, infrastructure assistance, and social adjustment and rural economic development amounted to $126.6 million in budgetary expenditures and $39.8 million in loans.[3]

There are some situations, however, in which the piper's paymaster doesn't always call the tune, and development planning seems to be one of them. Thus, ever since it became deeply involved in regional development schemes, the federal government has spoken of the need for regional planning and has attempted to persuade the individual Atlantic provinces to draw up their own plans and to cooperate in the elaboration of a regional plan.[4] Its success in Prince Edward Island is well known,[5] but in Nova Scotia two attempts have been aborted.*

Federal ambitions in the field of regional and national planning reached a peak in 1969 with the creation of the Department of Regional Economic Expansion.[6] The Department's policies, particularly its planning initiatives, received intense criticism; it encountered great difficulty in securing the cooperation of federal, as well as provincial, agencies and experienced repeated internal upheaval.[7] These reverses, together with Ottawa's traditional difficulty in resisting provincial pressures to support on an *ad hoc* basis whatever projects seem intrinsically desirable,[8] led to the gradual abandonment of the planning focus. Instead, the regional development strategy concentrated on three broad programs:

(i) The industrial development program seeks to create new productive employment by encouraging industry to invest in the slow-growth regions of the country.

(ii) The infrastructure assistance program seeks to complement industrial development activity by helping selected centres in these slow-growth regions to develop the community services and facilities re-

December 2, 1971) and Len Poetschke (*The Financial Post,* February 13, 1971) have criticized Ottawa for failing to involve local citizens of the region in development planning and for planning "from the top down."

* - The first, Voluntary Planning Board's *First Plan for Economic Development to 1968* (Halifax: Queen's Printer, 1966), was an interesting attempt at integrating grass roots and agency planning, but was virtually ignored by the government. The second, by the Cabinet Secretariat for Planning and Programs, was heavily criticized by federal officials and was abandoned after the change of provincial government in 1970.

quired to make them attractive as sites for commercial and industrial investment.

(iii) The rural development and social adjustment program seeks both to improve incomes in rural areas through more efficient resource utilization, and to help people gain access to new employment opportunities through various social development opportunities.[9]

As applied to Nova Scotia, and specifically to Port Hawkesbury and Bridgewater, these programs permit the federal government to assist industry in any part of the province and to provide infrastructure support in the Strait of Canso region, which is designated a "special area". Infrastructure projects at the Strait included construction of the highways connecting Point Tupper and Highway 4 and Port Hawkesbury and the Trans-Canada Highway; paving of roads in Point Tupper; servicing of the Port Hawkesbury light industrial park; and feasibility studies, including the Project 3.9 study which led to the design of the school and community centre projects. Bridgewater benefited from the industrial incentives scheme and a special highways agreement which permitted federal participation in the construction of Trunk 103, an important transportation link.[10] Other federal programs, such as those administered by Central Mortgage and Housing Corporation, also play a part in regional development, but those managed by DREE are generally considered the most important.

The federal regional development programs, although they are significant, clearly do not give Ottawa a controlling voice in development policy; they permit the federal government to influence policy. It can encourage certain activities; curb and even veto others; but it cannot control or direct. Ottawa's circumscribed role is attributable in part to political factors which limit its expenditures in the region; in part, to organizational problems in its key agency; and in part, to the reluctance of other agencies to be coordinated. But it is attributable basically to constitutional factors. The provinces are responsible under section 92 of the British North America Act for such matters as "local works and undertakings", "property and civil rights", crown lands, forests and minerals, and "generally all matters of a purely local or private nature." Consequently, they have welcomed Ottawa's contributions to regional development, but have ensured that "primary responsibility for the initiation and implementation of projects remained with the provinces."[11] The federal government found that its main functions were "limited to cost-sharing, policy coordination and the provision of technical and specialist services, and, where required, to supplement the comparatively less substantial staff resources of the provinces."[12] It is equally restricted in the field of community development where, despite numerous federal programs, overall control of municipal affairs is retained by the Province. Even its capacity to curb or veto provincial policies by witholding assistance would impede determined provincial politicians only in very large-scale projects like the Fundy tidal project or perhaps the building of the common-user dock at Mulgrave.

Provincial policy, then, is the keystone of Nova Scotia's industrial development program. The policies of the municipal and federal governments are necessary but essentially supportive. That being the case, the problem of why the Province failed to create and implement a more effective development policy for Nova Scotia in general and for the Strait and Bridgewater in particular must now be explored.

Neither a Will . . .

In broad terms, the provincial government's failure can be attributed to:

(a) apprehension on the part of successive governments that the Nova Scotia public would not support a planned approach to industrial development, and

(b) lack of an administrative structure capable of providing integrated, flexible policy and operational support for a comprehensive development program.

Just as a town like Bridgewater discovers that planning for development closes off opportunities for specific elements of the community, so does the Province. Roy George's study of Industrial Estates Limited illustrates this process and its effects. In his view, political considerations led IEL to abandon a policy, found effective elsewhere, of creating "well-designed, well-located industrial estates with advance factories" in favour of providing sites and buildings to suit clients' preferences.

> Pre-planned industrial estates would have to be built in a very few selected locations in the province and political pressures would immediately be exerted by those areas which felt neglected. Also, should an estate including advance factories lie idle for any length of time, political scorn will be heaped upon the developer, and taking such a risk requires more political courage than politicians and their offspring often possess. It is easier to sit back and wait until a client commits himself than to prepare in advance, even if such advance preparation is beneficial to the development of the province.[13]

Social as well as economic benefits would have followed from advance preparation of industrial estates. Some idea of educational needs could have been obtained in advance and provided for in an orderly fashion. Municipalities like those in the Bridgewater area would not have been faced with a sudden critical expansion of the school population.[14] Manpower and labour officials could have made some preparations in advance for training demands of new industry and could have drawn on their knowledge of the composition of the labour force to advise on location decisions. Construction of industrial facilities, instead of sparking local booms, might have been used to even out fluctuations in local economies. Local community planning would certainly have advanced. Above all, advance preparation of industrial estates would have permitted the Province to more effectively guide economic development and would have encouraged development of a general plan for Nova Scotia.

It is impossible to show conclusively today that fifteen years ago the provincial government would have lacked broad public support for a development policy that spelled out the future role of specific communities. As George has illustrated, however, the impression is very strong that destructive parochialism in the province has convinced politicians that this was so and is so. The Port Hawkesbury case study suggests this, as does the continual mainland resentment of Cape Breton and provincial resentment of Halifax-Dartmouth. A fear of being specific has inevitably crippled planning efforts.

In considering the socio-political climate during the period discussed in the case studies, it must be remembered that the Nova Scotia community has developed an increasingly complex social, political, and economic system over the last twenty-five years. A relatively detailed account of this process is presented in the report of the Graham Royal Commission and it will not be dealt with at length here. It is, however, worth while drawing out a few salient points. In the economy itself, for example, employment in primary industries (agriculture, forestry, fishing, trapping, and mining) fell from 24.7 per cent of the total labour force in 1951 to 7.7 per cent in 1971. The service sector,* on the other hand, grew from 49.5 per cent in 1951 to 63.2 per cent in 1971.[15] A significant feature of change in the labour force was the entry of a large number of women into the working world. This, in itself, has extensive implications from the point of view of provision of services by governments and the type of employment offered in the community. Similarly, the shift from primary to service industries brings with it a change in the composition of the labour force, including an increased employment of professionals in the province and consequent need for the kinds of services required by professionals of which the most obvious is improvement in the educational system. Another indicator of increased complexity in the Nova Scotia community has been the pattern of urban settlement that has developed between 1951 and 1971. Although Nova Scotia, unlike the other Canadian provinces, experienced very little growth in urban areas over the period,* the proportion of urban-oriented settlement

* - The service sector comprises members of the labour force working in transportation, trade, finance, community, and personal services, public and administration, and defense.
* - 54.5 per cent of the population in Nova Scotia lived in urban areas in 1951 and, in 1971, 56.7 per cent lived in urban areas (Graham Report, II. 2-14).

increased significantly. Rural farm population dropped significantly, but rural non-farm population rose by 16 per cent during the period 1966-71. As the *Graham Report* points out, this growth occurred in six counties near urban centres or points of development such as Port Hawkesbury. The *Report* suggests that "the implications of this trend upon provincial municipal government structures, should it continue, will be very great. It will increase the area over which the demand for urban-type services will develop, and will thereby increase the need for effective planning and for efficient implementation of plans."[16]

Attending the developing complexities and sophistication of the Nova Scotia community were commensurate attitudes and approaches to economic development, although in Nova Scotia, as elsewhere, changes in attitudes did not always ride hand in hand with changes in the province's economic situation. For example, during the early part of the period being studied there is a tendency to focus exclusively upon the need for investment to "create jobs". Once the impact of investment is felt, however, the pattern of concern appears to change and become fragmented. Groups closely related to the business sector continue, in general, to support developmental objectives. But other groups, particularly those for whom the benefits of investments are less obvious, or perhaps even negative, are more inclined to question the social utility of investment. In the most recent period, still further groups have questioned the effects of major industrial investments on the environment. Because these groups are so prominent today, there is a tendency to forget how recently they have emerged and how much every village and town in Nova Scotia wanted industrial development during the 1950s and most of the 1960s.

If it is assumed that public opinion did not support selective development policies, and probably opposed them, the fact that the decision to adopt a non-selective approach to development was a realistic political decision must also be accepted. It can, of course, be asked whether the people of Nova Scotia could not, like the people of New Brunswick, have been persuaded to accept major change, and whether the province's political leadership has been too timid. With hindsight, and the realization that the provincial government is accused of favouritism regardless of its intentions, a more forthright approach would appear to have been desirable.

. . . Nor a Way
A bolder stance on development would have involved more than political will. It would have depended on the right kind of administrative structure, one that could give integrated, flexible policy and operational support.* The chief deficiencies of the provincial civil

* - Here the contrast with New Brunswick is striking. Premier Robichaud's commitment to the Equal Opportunities Program attracted a competent core of civil

service have been:

(i) that, in the early years of development, at least, it lacked the experience and the competence to handle development policy; and

(ii) that it has resisted a coordinative approach to policy formation and implementation.

The governmental structure, particularly the administrative structure, which Nova Scotia possessed in the mid-1950s, although developing rapidly, was still a relatively simple construct.[17] J.M. Beck estimated that there were approximately 4,000 provincial government employees working in 14 departments. Comparatively speaking, these agencies were small in size; and this, in Beck's view, complicated "the business of administration, since, to all appearances, some Ministers have been far too prone to exercise supervision over the most minute details, thereby usurping the functions of their Deputies."[18] Subordination of the Deputy Ministers' function has undoubtedly contributed to the tendency of senior provincial civil servants to take a narrow view of their role and be reluctant to enter into policy-oriented joint activities with other administrative officials, except where designated to do so by political leaders. It has also contributed to the fragmentation and isolationism within provincial agencies that will be discussed below. The experience of the last five years is obviously one of adaptation to change and an approach to a more complex system of administration - as in the creation of the Department of Development to coordinate various types of development activity; in the abortive creation of a central policy structure; and in the later emergence of potential central policy structures. Unfortunately, this has come at the expense of, and in many respects too late for, towns like Port Hawkesbury and Bridgewater, which have experienced the most spectacular growth in the province.

In examining the province's administrative capability in the development field, the Department of Municipal Affairs and the various agencies concerned with economic development have been of paramount interest, but the part of other agencies must also be borne in mind as must the overall integration of agency activities and policies. Consequently, this discussion will consider the role and operation of the Department of Municipal Affairs and development agencies in some detail, will refer briefly to other agencies, and then will consider Nova Scotia's experience with central policy structures.

servants to the province. See Ralph R. Krueger, "The Provincial-Municipal Government Revolution in New Brunswick", *Canadian Public Administration*, XIII 1, p. 51.

Since economic development is the mainspring, the agencies operating in that field will be the first examined. The most important of these are the Department of Development - formerly the Department of Trade and Industry - and Industrial Estates Limited. Of some interest, however, are the Voluntary Planning Board and several other authorities responsible for encouraging specific types of development.

Industrial Estates Limited was established in 1957 to promote "diversification and development of industrial activity in Nova Scotia,"[19] or, as George has put it, "simply to create jobs."[20] Its structure, mandate, and mode of operation have led it to act independently, making investment decisions with scant regard to their social consequences. A crown corporation, it is under little obligation to cooperate with other government agencies. The Province, in fact, is committed to permit IEL "to operate as an autonomous corporation, free from control by, or interference from the Province", so long as it adheres to the general policy provisions of the IEL agreement.[21] These require that IEL "will not knowingly assist in the establishment of an industry . . . which will endanger any similar industry already existing or operating within Nova Scotia" and provide safeguards against the Province unwittingly permitting two of its agencies to assist the same company.[22] None of them require IEL to undertake advance planning of development activity, either on its own initiative or in conjunction with other government agencies.

Once in operation, IEL evolved a responsibility for attracting light industry to the province, leaving jurisdiction over the development of heavy industry to the Department of Trade and Industry. Thus, IEL was responsible for Michelin's location at Bridgewater, but seems to have had little to do with the Strait of Canso.[23] Within this rather loose framework, IEL appears to have had a free hand, constrained to a degree by government preferences, but more frequently influenced by the policies of federal agencies and the needs of prospective clients. It did not, apparently, develop "a very rigorous approach to industrial development."

No one has ever refined the early guidelines to an industrial strategy to determine the types of industry which could most easily be attracted to Nova Scotia or which could make the most beneficial contribution to the province's overall development. It is ironic that the 1971 Annual Report of IEL, probably the most cautious and even pessimistic of any of their reports, contains the first real sign of IEL's coming to grips with the nature of its task and the need for a logical approach to it . . . .

It apparently took a bad year and a new president to prod the board of directors to do some basic thinking in the absence of a government policy, with respect to the province's industrial development. Instead of an industrial strategy, there seems to have been simply an acceptance of the general need for more industry of any type. . . .24

Assigned a mammoth task in a highly competitive field, yet given a miniscule staff,[25] IEL emphasized the promotion of Nova Scotia as a manufacturing location. It spent most of its resources in advertising and promotional visits to possible clients. According to George, its record in establishing credit-worthiness compared well with that of similar agencies elsewhere in Canada.[26] But its assessment of enterprise viability, as the Deuterium and Clairtone cases demonstrated, frequently failed, partly because the company possessed too small a staff and did not call on the expertise of other provincial agencies, but also because its risk-taking philosophy and politically inspired secretiveness led it to play down the value of obtaining outside assessments.

Perhaps the most disruptive effects of IEL activities stem from its determination to conduct its operations in secret. These have been reported elsewhere,[27] so that here it is only necessary to note George's summary of the company's relations with other provincial agencies:

In the early days, it seemed to get along quite well with the Department of Trade and Industry, and paid tribute to help it had received from that department. In the middle and late 1960's, however, relationships with that and some other departments were not good, and IEL dealt directly and almost exclusively with the cabinet. With the change in presidency in 1970 and the change in government soon after, the relationships between IEL and the government departments were altered drastically. The new government seemed determined that development activities previously carried on by various departments and organizations should be coordinated. Soon after he took office, the new Premier, Gerald A. Regan, saw it necessary to confirm that IEL did not act independently of the government. A new Department of Development was established, and the Minister, Ralph F. Fiske, said that it would "be providing 'back-up' material needed by IEL in promoting secondary industry . . . IEL has been asked . . . to be more selective in the industries which it attracts." Further, he confirmed that "IEL will be functioning under the policies established by the government and at the present time, which point, that has never existed before, is that there is communication between IEL and the Department of Development which did not exist with the previous government or any other government." The new president of IEL, Finlay MacDonald, welcomed this arrangement, declaring that ". . . IEL cannot, should not, and will not exist alone any longer." His successor, Dean W. Salsman, reported that ". . . physical proximity allows IEL to consult frequently with this department [the Department of Development which was accommodated in the same office building as IEL].As well, IEL relies heavily on expertise available from the Nova Scotia Research Foundation and other government agencies. IEL intends to regularly communicate and consult with the Cape Breton Development Corporation in matters of common interest." Perhaps the days of IEL's glorious isolation have ended.28

It will be noted, however, that IEL's improved relations with other agencies have occurred primarily in the industrial development field. Contacts with social development agencies seem to be nearly as limited as ever.* As IEL's secretary, Frank M. LeTourneau, points out,

*Integration with the Department of Development has entailed some improved second-hand contact, as will be seen below.

IEL has no interest in the social development of communities.[29]

Under its orginal mandate, the Department of Trade and Industry was assigned functions that encouraged a stance as isolationist as that of IEL.[30] The promotion of the province as a site for location of heavy industry was its chief responsibility, and this included encouragement of local industrial commissions and development of industrial parks. In this capacity it developed the Point Tupper Industrial Park. The Department was also responsible for tourism, certain aspects of recreation, and acquisition and development of economic data. It was assigned no responsibilities that would encourage it to participate in planning overall development strategy. That function was entrusted to the Voluntary Economic Planning Board.[31]

Originally established under the Minister of Finance and Economics, the Voluntary Economic Planning Board had the "general function" of assisting and advising the Minister in "the development and implementation of measures to increase the rate of economic growth of the province by means of voluntary economic planning."[32] More specifically, it was to "coordinate the plans of the various sectors of the economy and, based on these plans, produce a plan for the whole economy of the province for recommendation to the Minister as one which the government might adopt."[33] But the Board did not possess the authority that its terms of reference would warrant. In particular, it had no power to coordinate the activity of planning in the various sectors of the economy and lacked the persuasive power to "stimulate and encourage" the carrying out of plans. It had no coercive power; it was not authorized to use financial persuasion; and it had no claim to coordinate those activities of the public sectors which affect the performance of private economic concerns.

Given these constraints, it is not surprising that the Board found itself in an anomalous situation. It could, and did, elicit the active support of the private sector in developing various studies of aspects of the economy and in developing a *First Plan* for the economic development of Nova Scotia,[34] but it had no power to ensure governmental cooperation, or even consideration of its proposals. This became evident when the *First Plan* was submitted and the Board found that little effort was made to implement or review it.

Encumbered with a mandate beyond its capabilities and rebuffed in its first attempts to grapple with the general problems of planning, VEP experienced a decline in reputation and support. The election of the Regan administration in October 1970 seemed to herald its demise, for the Liberals viewed it as a partisan device of the retiring government.[35] That it was not eliminated was probably due to two factors. First, the Board had been successful in drawing together key representatives of the private sector and had given them a vehicle for communicating with the government. In other words, it provided a formal contact between government and interest groups. Some, at least, valued this point of access and considered it sufficiently useful to be maintained. Second, the Board itself was concerned by its failure and established a subcommittee to review its activities and recommend a change in function. Concluding that "it is clear that the original concept of VEP . . . is no longer applicable", but that "the concept of involvement of the private sector in planning has, in VEP, illustrated an excellent potential", the committee suggested that "an active and more effective participation of the private sector in overall development planning should be the basis for a revised role for VEP."[36] Emphasizing the need for full government commitment to a new role, and the need for directing staff energies solely to supporting the various sector committees,* the committee recommended that VEP undertake:

> to provide for the effective involvement of the private sector in development planning. Within this general definition, two specific functions are seen:
>
> a - to facilitate the identification of problems by the private sector and to relate appropriate private and public resources in an attempt to resolve these problems;
>
> b- to involve the private sector in the analysis of government planning proposals during the process of their development, and prior to final approval.[37]

The committee's report was timely. In Opposition, the new government had strongly criticized the Stanfield-Smith approach to development, charging that poor coordination of responsible agencies had inhibited the preparation and application of a well-planned development strategy and had weakened the government's capacity to properly assess development proposals like those for Clairtone and Deuterium. This attack had been the most important part of their campaign, and once in power the Liberals were understandably anxious to reorganize the Province's development agencies. VEP's own proposal meshed with the government's thinking and the Board became a part of the new machinery for development.

The essence of the reorganization was incorporated in a 1971 amendment to the Public Service Act[38] that transferred to a renamed Department of Trade and Industry responsibility for administering the economic development policies of the Province[39] and for coordinating

---

* - Staff had been employed in preparing studies for other agencies beside VEP. With reorganization, several staff members were transferred to these other agencies, a change that was seen by some as a further weakening of the Board. In view of their previously divided responsibilities, it is doubtful whether this assessment is quite accurate.

the development activities of various departments.[40] The first provision, which gave to the Department of Development responsibilities undertaken both by its predecessor and the Department of Finance, included the transfer of Voluntary Planning from Finance to Development, and so strengthened the capacity of the Planning Board to influence Development policy.[41] The Department also assumed responsibility for carrying on the Province's relations with the federal Department of Regional Economic Expansion.[42] Later its responsibilities for tourism and recreation were transferred to two new departments, and its focus on planning and development was consequently reaffirmed. Closer liaison with the IEL staff was also established.[43]

The new arrangements, together with the consolidation of several lesser agencies,[44] are generally thought to have brought about a more effective coordination of development activity. The professional and information resources of Trade and Industry and Voluntary Economic Planning[45] have been consolidated and are said to be more effectively used by the new department and by IEL. Contact with the private sector is institutionalized through the integration of Voluntary Planning in the Development Department, and efforts to create a sound information base for development planning seem to be achieving some results.* There is an apparent appreciation of the broader effects of development reflected in Alex Harris' appointment as Strait Coordinator[46] and in the Department's involvement in the Cabinet Committee on Development, which will be discussed below.

The Regan government's approach to reorganization was, however, not entirely consistent. It failed to create a master plan for the province, and it exposed the government to charges similar to those that had previously troubled the Stanfield-Smith regime. In particular, development policy continued to be fragmented, but now because the Premier undertook responsibility for certain projects such as tidal power, oil development, and the proposed refineries at Mulgrave, while leaving the major part of development administration to his Minister, George Mitchell. On the whole, agency appreciation of the broader issues of development improved, but only marginally. Communication with agencies outside the development field itself seems to be limited, and both local governments and the public at large complain of continued secretiveness and unresponsiveness. By 1974, the Graham Commission was warning that "there is a great need for coherent, consistent and mutually supportive economic development policies."[47] In its view, the provincial government had achieved an effective reorganization of development agencies, but not related agencies, and it had made a major error in dismantling the

---

*-As, for example, in the preparation of economic profiles for the various counties.

embryo central policy structure left by the Smith government.

The most important of the non-development agencies in meeting the challenge of industrial expansion at the local level is the Department of Municipal Affairs. Established in 1935, the Department has traditionally defined its role narrowly. As recently as 1957, Beck described its objective as "to effect an improvement in the administration of municipal affairs, and, to that end, it supervises the borrowing of the local governments, regulates their sinking fund payments, prescribes a system of estimates, bookkeeping, and accounts for their use, and studies and advises upon the existing system of municipal administration."[48]

Although a Town Planning Act had been introduced in 1939,[49] its impact was negligible; "many people talked favourably about planning, but few municipal units possessed the determination and/or the capacity to act on their general planning convictions."[50] Since the Act relied heavily on the voluntary efforts of the municipalities, the Department's Community Planning Division (CPD) found itself playing an insignificant role, both within and outside the Department. As has been noted, the 1969 review of the Act brought about legislative revisions that made planning mandatory and enhanced the role of the CPD. Unfortunately, the CPD has had difficulty capitalizing on its enlarged mandate. A major problem has been the slowness with which the planning gospel has been accepted in the province.[51] It is still common to hear provincial and municipal officials express complete ignorance of the planning process, and there is a recurrent feeling that planning and development are at opposite extremes.[52]

Within the government, the Division has encountered additional difficulties. The Department of Municipal Affairs, until recently, has itself been slow to appreciate the desirability of coordinating the planning and budgeting functions of local governments, and, internally, reluctant to give the Division a major policy role. Other departments have been even less inclined to acknowledge the coordinative thrust of the revised Planning Act, and have generally ignored the Division's pleas for broader participation in decisions affecting local communities. Finally, the Division has been thwarted by a succession of major political decisions. The election of the Regan government brought the end of the Cabinet Secretariat on Planning and Priorities to which the Division had looked for support in developing a coordinated approach to provincial planning.[53] The appointment of the Graham Commission occasioned a great deal of delay at the provincial and municipal level, since it encouraged many administrators and politicians to put off - often quite legitimately - making major decisions until the Graham recommendations had been received and absorbed.

All of this took its toll on the Community Planning Division, bringing about staff depletion and eventually a loss of leadership. By 1974 the Division was barely performing the function of reviewing proposed municipal plans, and the Department as a whole was receiving intense criticism for its apparently inconsistent planning policies, inadequate staff, and disastrous slowness in processing proposed plans and by-laws. In the cautious language of the *Graham Report*, "a restructuring and redirection of the Department . . . have been imminent for a long time . . . The fragmentation of its services, the lack of internal and external communication, and its consequent inability to respond effectively in several areas, have been the Department's main weaknesses . . . Nowhere at the provincial government level is the need for reorganization and almost complete change in past and present approaches more apparent."[54]

As has been suggested in the two case studies, policy coordination between other agencies of the provincial government has been insignificant. This has been reflected in the application of contradictory policies in specific communities and is documented more fully in the report of the Graham Commission. The crux of the problem in the past has been the lack of a means of integrating and carrying out economic and social planning on a province-wide basis. In part, the lack of such a vehicle can be related to the difficulties of reconciling the objectives of development and planning. The perception of these as dichotomous has been a mistaken - but nevertheless formidable - barrier to achieving a more rational and sensible procedure for relating large-scale social and economic demands to one another and to the physical resources of the Province. A second barrier, however, has been the difficulty the Province has experienced in introducing central policy structures for review and planning purposes. That problem will now be examined in some detail.

Although the origins of current problems are deeply rooted and go back a considerable distance in time, some explanation can be derived from recent history. Nova Scotia was not initially laggard in setting up a provincial cabinet-level Priorities and Planning Committee. Nor did it deny the Committee a competent and dedicated staff. A Planning Secretariat was created in May 1969[55] and proceeded to prepare a comprehensive development plan for consideration by Ottawa as part of its regional economic development policy.[56]

The Secretariat, however, soon encountered difficulties. Within the civil service there was a good deal of apprehension that the Secretariat would take over the policy advisory role of line departments, a fear that Secretariat staff members seemed to encourage with a rather heavy-handed approach to relations with line departments. There was considerable hostility between the Secretariat and established agencies.

The defeat of the Smith government in October 1970 also spelled the end of the Secretariat. The Liberal Opposition had formed an extremely unfavourable view of it and, when they moved to the government benches, decided that the Secretariat should be disbanded, saying that it had not been "designed as the correct vehicle for planning, and was not using public funds in the best possible manner."[57] Its passage was unregretted within the civil service and senior members of the service still recall its brief life with distaste. It is probable that any attempt to create a new Secretariat to coordinate central policy discussions would encounter strong opposition within the senior civil service.*

Despite its rejection of the Secretariat, the Liberal government found it necessary to maintain an agency at the centre in charge of liaison and special studies. Calling government "the most inefficient, poorly organized major business existing in Nova Scotia", Premier Gerald Regan indicated that departments would be reorganized and that their policy recommendations would receive pre-Cabinet review by a "counter-bureaucracy" of special assistants.[58] Initially, the centre of this activity was the Cabinet Office under the Secretary of the Cabinet, Fred Drummie. For a time this office appeared to be emerging as another general review and coordination body. It possessed a small staff of professionals and engaged in a number of planning-oriented activities and special studies. It too, however, encountered opposition within the senior civil service and possibly at the political level. Its failure became public in April 1972 when Eugene Chatterton, a senior official in the new structure, resigned, saying that "the provincial government's thinking is all screwed up"; federal-provincial attempts at joint planning were valueless; and the Province was no closer to a development plan than it had been a year earlier.[59]

In 1972 the Cabinet Office disappeared and became the Department of the Executive Council, which has more recently reverted to its old title of Executive Council Office.[60] After the departure of Fred Drummie in late 1972, the Executive Council Office, under Innis MacLeod, with a small staff, resumed the fairly modest role it had played under the Stanfield and Smith governments, namely:

a) examination of submissions to the Executive Council,
b) preparation of draft Orders-in-Council,
c) registration, certification and filing of Orders-in-Council,
d) maintaining liaison with the several departments and agencies of the Province,
e) providing secretarial services for the Executive Council,
f) making studies of administrative or policy matters,
g) providing chairmen, secretaries, or members for interdepartmental committees, and
h) keeping track of pertinent administrative and policy matters in other jurisdictions.[61]

* - An impression created by periodic discussions with a number of senior officials in the Nova Scotia service.

Today the major coordinative body in the provincial government is the Treasury Board, which performs the functions generally assigned Treasury Boards but also appears to exercise more general powers, similar to those wielded by the federal Treasury Board prior to the development of the Cabinet committee system and the expansion of the Privy Council Office in the early 1960s. As well, considerable control has been exercised directly by the Premier's office, but that office lacks the staff to carry out policy coordination on the scale normally considered desirable. Other than the Treasury Board, one major Cabinet committee, the Development Committee, was established in mid-1973 and came to exercise some influence over economic policy. It consists of four ministers - including Finance, Municipal Affairs, Environment, and Development - and such staff support as is needed is supplied from the departments they represent. The Committee appears to be well regarded within Cabinet and the senior bureaucracy and may represent the beginning of a final and successful attempt to establish a central coordinative body within the administrative structure. Recently it has been joined by another Cabinet committee working in the education and social policy field. For the moment, however, the fact remains that Nova Scotia policy is highly fragmented, and the provincial agencies are slow to integrate their activities with one another's, or with those of other governments.

This weakness has been recognized by the Graham Commission, which has criticized the Province's reversion "to an *ad hoc* approach which must have detrimental implications for regional-municipal planning and for the Province's capacity to respond quickly and effectively to major problems and opportunities."[62] The Commission has recommended the restructuring of Cabinet committees and their support staff along the lines adopted by other provinces. Whether the Commission's recommendations will be adopted is still uncertain.

In summary, the Province's capacity to appreciate the effects of economic development on affected local governments has been limited by the fragmented nature of its administrative structure; the self-imposed isolation of its major agencies; and the absence of a central policy structure supporting Cabinet itself. Its tardiness in meeting the problems of development can be attributed to the same factors.

V. BROADENING THE SCOPE OF DEVELOPMENT PLANNING

Bridgewater and Port Hawkesbury Varieties of Development

Two case studies have introduced the effects of industrial development in Port Hawkesbury and Bridgewater and have allowed consideration of how both communities responded to the changes that came with the new industry. As well, they have given a view of the complex relationships that evolve out of the application of provincial development policy; relationships that affect all three levels of government.

A number of conclusions have been drawn from the case studies, reflecting, first, the social infrastructure needs of communities experiencing industrial development, and, second, the administrative and policy requirements of an industrial development program. In the following paragraphs these conclusions will be elaborated still further and then suggestions will be made as to how they may be applied to future policy. The Bridgewater-Port Hawkesbury experience indicates that, assuming no exceptional socio-economic or geographic circumstances, five variables are critical determinants of the capacity of communities to absorb development investment. Three of these variables relate to the nature of the community itself; the fourth relates to the type of investment experienced; and the fifth, to the role of external political systems. The community-related variables are:

1. The demographic features of the host community;

2. The inventory of public utilities, community facilities, and social services possessed by the host community at the start of population influx; and

3. The political and administrative capacity of the host community.

Bridgewater, for example, was a more complex, diversified, and sophisticated community than was Port Hawkesbury. It had a larger population at the time the Michelin investment decision was made. It also had been a recognized commercial and business centre for decades. It consequently possessed many services and amenities that were lacking in the Port Hawkesbury area. These included such essentials as a secure water supply and community facilities such as meeting places, schools, and so on. The community itself was large enough to absorb a sudden, but not overwhelming, increase in population. It possessed a structure of community organizations which was sufficiently stable and diversified to permit newcomers to establish themselves without experiencing the intense isolation and sense of alienation that was a prominent feature of Port Hawkesbury's development. The Bridgewater business community, too, was more diversified than that of Port Hawkesbury and, in many respects, more capable of meeting "outsiders" on their own ground.

The Bridgewater community, particularly the business community, had a perception of itself as aggressive and adaptable to change. It is difficult to determine whether the Port Hawkesbury community possessed a similar approach, but the general impression conveyed by numerous interviews is that the community at large, during the early '50s and '60s, tended to have little confidence in itself and to look to senior levels of government to secure the type of investment needed to keep the community alive. Even the Four Counties Development Association, which has been given some of the credit for starting the developments at Point Tupper, was primarily interested in only one industry, the pulp and paper mill, and withered away not long after its establishment.

When at attempt is made to assess the response to development of the local level of government, the conclusion is reached that Bridgewater demonstrated a capacity to adjust that was lacking at Port Hawkesbury. Bridgewater's apparent success has been attributed to various factors, including an effective leadership, the advice and assistance of an experienced and respected planner, a community spirit, and a sense of drive within the business community. There are other factors, as well. Local government did not have to grapple with as large a variety of decisions as did that in Port Hawkesbury. It was not coping with a radical, a total, change in its community. It did not suddenly find itself having to provide the basic services of an urban community. The relative scale of decision making, consequently, permitted greater freedom of action. It was probably because they were not preoccupied with the need to provide basic services that Bridgewater's civic and business leaders recognized, very early in the development experience, the need for social as well as economic planning for development. And out of this realization came the attempt to engage in a fairly sophisticated and locally dominated planning process.

A similar appreciation did not surface in Port Hawkesbury until after the first phase of industrial expansion. In Port Hawkesbury the local councils were apt to be overwhelmed by the process in which they were engaged. The town's proposed development plan drew attention to problems posed by "inadequate staff, not enough finances, little experience with rapid growth, and no means for dealing with such difficult but basic municipal responsibilities as helping people find adequate housing."[1] A close observer of the Port Hawkesbury scene suggests that municipal councils have been too trusting, particularly of other levels of government.

> They look(ed) to the civil servants at the various levels as being good guys; and they were very trusting . . . . I think they're often led into positions by government, trusting government all the way, and when the chips come down . . . .Right now I feel the government's letting them carry the can.[2]

The more sophisticated aspects of the planning process, particularly the attempt at citizen participation, did not make much headway until late in 1973. Then the feasibility study of the proposed school and community centre complex became an important experiment in citizen participation and led to a vastly increased public awareness of the utility of participation, the ramifications of which are still being felt. At this same time, Port Hawkesbury's Town Council itself acknowledged its incapacity to deal with other levels of government and large corporations, and began a campaign to appoint a local administrative official possessing some of the expertise needed to carry on negotiations with these bodies.[3]

Comparison of Port Hawkesbury and Bridgewater leads to one major generalization which, although obvious, is frequently ignored. That is:

The capacity of communities to absorb industrial development will vary with the size of their population and the complexity of their social, political and economic systems. The larger and more varied a community, the more easily will it adapt to the infusion of new people and new industries.

Later in this chapter an attempt will be made to apply this generalization to the formulation of a social policy paralleling industrial development strategy.

The fourth variable determining capacity to absorb development investment is *the nature of the industry introduced into the community.* The importance of this variable is illustrated dramatically by the comparison of Bridgewater and Port Hawkesbury. Though each community eventually acquired approximately the same number of permanent additional employees as a result of development, the fact that Point Tupper is a centre for heavy industry exposed Port Hawkesbury to two highly disruptive construction booms. Port

Hawkesbury and neighbouring communities were inundated by transient labour forces at the same time as they were attempting to adjust to a greatly enlarged permanent, or semi-permanent, community. The construction phase was traumatic. For Bridgewater construction was a point of minor stress, but generally a forerunner of affluence.

Again, it must be remembered that the nature of investment in the two communities was quite different. Bridgewater was to be the new home of a corporation with an unusual approach to its relations with the community and its work force. Of the companies established at Port Hawkesbury, only' Gulf, which went to some trouble to investigate the social climate of the Strait, appears to have taken a comparable view of these relationships. Furthermore, apart from the Michelin investment, Bridgewater's growth depended less on large-scale decisions by international corporations than it did on a number of relatively small decisions by local and national corporations. This type of investment decision is much more amenable to control by the locality than is the type of investment decision taken at the Strait. The latter rapidly becomes a matter of concern to provincial, federal, and even international spheres of government. Local capacity to influence the decisions varies inversely with the scale of the investment and the number of levels of government involved in the overall decision.

The final variable influencing absorptive capacity is the most complex, although it can be stated simply enough as the policies and capabilities of other governments. In the cases reviewed here other local governments, the provincial government, and the federal government were all involved in the development process. Of these, the provincial government, because of its particular responsibilities, played a critically important role.

The Province's failure to develop a comprehensive industrial development policy has been attributed to:

(i) government fears that the socio-political climate would not support a planned approach to development, and

(ii) lack of an administrative structure capable of providing integrated, flexible policy and operational support for a comprehensive development program.

In other words, the Province has been afraid to spell out a development policy and, until recently at least, lacked the administrative capability to do so. Administrative incapacity is attributed to:

(i) lack of experience and expertise in the development field during the early years of industrial expansion, and

(ii) internal resistance to coordination of policy formation and implementation.

These factors are at the heart of the conditions that have been described. Until they are resolved, it can be expected that the Bridgewater and Port Hawkesbury experience will be repeated again and again.

The Possibilities of Development Policy
Earlier the increasing complexity of the Province's socio-economic and political system was referred to, and a trend towards policy coordination and a developing expertise in the provincial civil service were noted. These trends will presumably continue and lead eventually to greater coordination of provincial policy and a more explicit public statement of development objectives. Consequently it is worth while considering the implications of the Bridgewater-Port Hawkesbury experience and attempting to place them in a framework that has policy relevance, using as a base the generalization that a community's absorptive capacity will vary with the size of its population and the complexity of its social, political, and economic systems. On this base an attempt will be made to build a series of policy suggestions aimed primarily at the provincial government, but also at other levels of government and industry itself.

1. General policy requirements
Agency isolation and policy fragmentation have spawned a development policy that is preoccupied with the creation of jobs and is not supported by appropriate social and community development measures. Modern industrial development demands a broader approach, one that augments the traditional incentive systems, marketing techniques, and vetting procedures of development agencies with:

(a) a recognition that the social consequences of development will be as great, if not greater, than the economic consequences; and

(b) a consequent commitment to spell out the details of development planning in a comprehensive provincial master plan.

Implicit in this approach is a willingness to accept the political consequences of development policy (including selection of development areas); a recognition of the need for administrative coordination and the full involvement of virtually all agencies of government in development planning. It involves, as well, public participation in development planning and implies a freer relationship

between levels of government. Important subordinate features of such an approach would include:
  (a) acceptance of the view that the capacity of communities to absorb new industry will vary;
  (b) a willingness, in consequence: (i) to treat each development situation as unique; (ii) to formally recognize the special circumstances of each; and (iii) regardless of prevailing policy, to provide each special development area with the human and financial resources necessary to permit it to cope with development in a reasonable manner; and
  (c) recognition of the need to accord to the local level the fullest possible scope for decision making.

2. Development policy at the provincial level
An approach such as the one suggested would impose the greatest burden at the provincial level. The first element in a provincial strategy would be promotion within provincial agencies of a multilateral appreciation of the effect of change. That is, all agencies of the provincial government that, in any way, are involved with creating the conditions under which a community experiences change should be alert to the possible effects that that change will have on the community. Administratively, this would require the creation of central policy structures and a much higher degree of advance planning and planning coordination than now exists. Central planning, however, can lead to as many abuses as it cures. Fragmentation of policy and confusion of purpose can be replaced by rigid adherence to a theoretically attractive master plan that in reality is destructive of the communities it is meant to serve. True coordination and responsive planning must avoid these perils, placing great stress on meaningful communication with the general public.

Acceptance of the view that communities have different capacities for absorbing development would require, at the administrative level, an extensive use of task groups to assess the needs of individual communities. From time to time secondment of personnel to administratively weak municipalities would be necessary, as might the acceptance of expertise from the federal level. A regional field system like that now in effect at the Strait or that proposed by the Graham Commission would be essential.

At the policy level, the approach would require much greater flexibility, particularly in the municipal government field, than is now the case. Local development grants, for example, would cut across traditional grant structures. Allowing a greater degree of local decision making would inevitably complicate the application of general policies. Closer alignment with federal policies would also be desirable.

There are quite profound implications in a provincial policy that admits, first, that not all communities are equally capable of absorbing change and, second, that weaker communities must be helped to make up their deficiencies. It would mean that the Province would have to go far beyond providing physical infrastructure. The Province would be concerned with social infrastructure, in the fullest sense of the term. Thus, where communities that are not complex in structure are expected to receive massive investment, a provincial strategy for investment should provide special assistance to develop the degree of complexity needed to absorb a population infusion. A community such as Bridgewater, which has a well developed community structure, needs far less assistance than a community like Port Hawkesbury; there should be no inconsistency in providing the latter with amenities not provided the former. These would include physical amenities, such as community centres, that would create a physical capacity to encourage and sustain community groups and so give the town character, a sense of identity, and an ability to receive and adapt to newcomers. Just as important, they would include professional assistance, not simply at the local government level, but in all aspects of community activity. In Port Hawkesbury the various churches play a very important role in this respect, providing facilities and the spiritual assistance needed to help a disparate population become a community.

Fundamental to all of this would be an abandonment of the stance provincial authorities have traditionally taken toward their "creatures", the municipalities. In general, with the periodic exception of the CPD, Nova Scotia provincial agencies have taken a narrow regulatory approach to their relations with the municipalities that is often described politely as "paternalistic" and, in moments of stress, as "arbitrary and domineering". Yet as these case studies suggest, there is frequently very little to support provincial claims to "know best" what is right for the municipalities. Bridgewater's officials, for example, frequently demonstrated that they were far more far-sighted and expeditious than their provincial colleagues. Even Port Hawkesbury with its limited administrative resources revealed an appreciation of regulatory needs that eluded officials in Halifax. In brief, paternalistic regulations must be supplanted by the understanding application of regulations and a supportive attitude to local attempts to achieve community-defined objectives.

Recognition of the idiosyncratic features of development, however, should not preclude an attempt to create a general development strategy for the province as a whole. Such an attempt is inherent in the idea of creating a development coordinating group at the central policy level and in preparing a master plan for the province. The investment community, the local community, and particularly local and provincial governments need to be able to anticipate the direction of future change. General strategies and master plans cannot be ultra-specific but can guide the general pattern of investment decisions, both on the part of business and on the part of government.

3. The role of the federal government

Given the preponderant authority of the provincial government in the industrial development and local government fields, Ottawa will continue to play an essentially supportive role. In the light of the need to increase the scope of local decision making, this is probably appropriate.

However, the federal government could make more effective use of its position. By achieving better coordination of its own programs, meshing its policies more closely with those of the provinces, and broadening its own development philosophy, the senior government could facilitate policy making and provide for anticipatory, rather than reactive, planning.

4. Community development

The most exciting consequences of a broadened development policy would be found at the local level. While the main onus for developing a suitable development strategy rests with the Province, the local community need by no means wait for guidance from the Province. In fact, as the Bridgewater experience shows, the stronger the community's own sense of capacity to meet the challenge of development, the better its chances of eventually coping successfully with it. Here again, the need to provide for complexity suggests a suitable goal for local officials as well as those at the provincial level.

Various models are available for improving the quality and extent of local government involvement in community development. Bridgewater's experience with its development commission is one, although it needs to be supplemented by a more effective process of citizen participation; another is suggested by the experience of Pictou County, and a third by the recent innovations at Port Hawkesbury and the Strait. All permit the community to obtain a clearer view of the course and implications of development and provide opportunities for influencing decision makers operating outside the local area. Programs designed to stimulate local interest and understanding, like Verge's planning blitz at Bridgewater, serve the same purpose, although, to be effective, they require (1) that officials thoroughly understand their roles; and (2) that continuing organizational support exists to sustain the interest they generate.

Professional administrative support during the development cycle is also essential to the local government confronting massive change. Whether seconded from other governments or hired by the local authorities - with the financial assistance of senior governments - professionals are required to upgrade the municipality's administrative system; to help the local community make its own appraisal of the economic effects of development; to assist in community planning; and to anticipate and help provide social needs. Given this type of assistance, local officials not only find that they are better able to provide new services, but that they are more effective in securing the community's interests in negotiations with other governments and with industry.

Hand in hand with extending the community's part in development and with the acquisition of professional support, is the need for a better understanding of the development process itself. As these case studies show, local communities and their representatives tend to be overwhelmed by the glamour of development. To some extent, fuller understanding is provided through planning blitzes and professional staff, but something more is necessary. Study groups, seminars conducted by professionals and individuals with practical experience, and, where possible, visits to communities that have experienced development would all help the community take a level-headed approach to the opportunities and challenges before them. Advance study, for example, can assist the municipality to anticipate the course of development and thus to influence the pattern of decision making at the provincial level. It can help define the terms of the relationships between new corporate community citizens and both the Province and the locality. Simply by insisting that management study the social ramifications of the company's investment decision, for example, the town can do a good deal to ensure its own peaceful cohabitation with the new industry.

To respond to the challenge of investment in the fashion suggested, local government must be able to work within a provincial policy framework that is enlightened, broadly based, and supportive. A provincial approach that focuses primarily on regulating the municipalities, that is inflexible and fragmented, and that seems to reflect a fear of local autonomy and public involvement will be self-defeating. Within it, the objective of improving the lot of local residents is lost sight of and industrial expansion becomes an end in itself. Through the experience of towns like Bridgewater and Port Hawkesbury, Nova Scotia will, it is hoped, achieve a humanistic approach to development.

REFERENCES ⸱

I. Introduction

1 - See Philip Mathias, *Forced Growth* (Toronto: James Lewis and Samuel, 1971); Roy E. George, *The Life and Times of Industrial Estates Limited* (Halifax: Institute of Public Affairs, Dalhousie University, 1974); and Michael Bradfield *Provincial Development Corporations* (Halifax: Atlantic Province Economic Council, 1973).

2 - The Bridgewater town plan states that Michelin expects to employ 1,200 to 1,300 by the end of 1975 (*Town of Bridgewater: Municipal Development Plan* [Bridgewater: Lunenburg County District Planning Commission, March 1975], p. 16); Point Tupper is said to employ approximately 1,200 (Nova Scotia Department of Development. *County Profile: Richmond* [Halifax: 1974] p. 22).

II. Bridgewater: The Entrepreneurial Approach

1 - Nova Scotia. Royal Commission on Education, Public Services and Provincial-Municipal Relations, *Report (the Graham Report)* (Halifax: Queen's Printer, 1974) II. 18-31.

2 - J.E. Defebaugh, *History of the Lumber Industry of America* (Chicago: The American Lumberman, 1906), pp. 249, 259, 187.

3 - Nova Scotia Department of Development, *County Profile: Lunenburg* (Halifax: 1974), p. 66.

4 - *Ibid.*, p. 45.

5 - Roy E. George, *A Leader and a Laggard: Manufacturing Industry in Nova Scotia, Quebec and Ontario,* (Toronto: University of Toronto Press, 1970) p. 114.

6 - Heritage Trust of Nova Scotia, *South Shore: Seasoned Timbers* (Halifax: 1974), p. 70.

7 - *Ibid.*

8 - Geoffrey Stevens, *Stanfield* (Toronto: McClelland & Stewart, 1973).

9 - *Ibid.*

10 - Industrial Commissions Act, *Revised Statutes of Nova Scotia* (RSNS), 1967, c. 137, s. 10.

11 - Interview with John Hirtle.

12 - *Ibid.*

13 - Interview with Frank M. LeTourneau, Secretary, IEL, July 10, 1974. See also *Financial Post,* December 19, 1970.

14 - *The 4th Estate,* Halifax, May 24, 1973.

15 - *Ibid.,* Verge quoted.

16 - *Ibid.*

17 - *Ibid.*

18 - *Bridgewater Bulletin,* April 19, 1972.

19 - Confidential source.

20 - *Bridgewater Development Plan and Zoning By-law,* June 1973 (*Plan and by-law,* 1973), p. 2.

21 - *Ibid.,* p. 4.

22 - *Ibid.*

23 - *The 4th Estate,* May 24, 1973.

24 - *Ibid.*

25 - *Ibid.*

26 - Robert Manthorne was later elected to Council, in 1974.

27 - *Plan and by-law,* 1973, p. 1.

28 - Interview with Lawrence Keddy, Department of Municipal Affairs, Community Planning Division, May 21, 1974.

29 - *Graham Report,* II. 6 - 287.

30 - A revised plan was submitted to the Community Planning Division in March 1975. See Lunenburg County District Planning Commission, *Municipal Development Plan: Town of Bridgewater,* March 1975.

31 - See Municipality of the District of Lunenburg, *Annual Report of Warden Charles E. Walters,* January 1975.

32 - DREE film, "From the Middle of Nowhere".

33 - The Bridgewater Municipal Development Plan (p. 14) claims that the town's service area extends from the eastern portion of Shelburn County to the western portion of the District of Chester. The Department of Development describes the service area as extending from Mill Village on the west, to Western Shore on the east, and Springhill on the north (*County Profile: Lunenburg,* p. 45).

34 - See *County Profile: Lunenburg,* p. 9-11.

III. **Port Hawkesbury: Development and Dependence**

1 - Interview with former Mayor, Arthur J. Langley, Jr., June 26, 1974.

2 - Rev. Douglas Campbell, *Industrial Development of Conference, Port Hawkesbury, November 19-20, 1971, Proceedings* (mimeo., 1971), p. 2.

3 - See Nova Scotia, Legislative Assembly, *Debates,* February 5, 1959, pp. 61-62 (Henry Hicks); February 9, 1959, p. 188 (Robert Stanfield), February 9, 1961, p. 99 (Earl W. Urquhart).

4 - An excellent summary of the company's development from 1960 to 1970, and of other industrial development at Point Tupper in the period, is contained in a report prepared by Economic Consultants Limited for the Nova Scotia

Government Cabinet Secretariat on Planning and Programs, entitled *Development Strategy for the Strait of Canso Area of Nova Scotia* (Charlottetown: 1970, mimeo.). Other data concerning total investment, production, and employment at Point Tupper were obtained from Nova Scotia Department of Municipal Affairs, Community Planning Division, *Strait of Canso: Area Information* (Halifax: 1973).

5 - Nova Scotia Department of Development, *County Profile: Richmond* (Halifax: 1974), p. 22.

6 - Nova Scotia Department of Development, *County Profile: Inverness* (Halifax: 1974), p. 16-17. Provincial average was $5,490.

7 - "Regional Development: Strait of Canso Area". An unsigned and undated draft, developed 1969-70, probably in the Community Planning Division, Department of Municipal Affairs, p. 3.

8 - Hon. Ralph Fiske, *Industrial Development Conference,* p. 21.

9 - "Regional Development: Strait of Canso Area", pp. 4, 11.

10 - Confidential interview.

11 - Canadian Bechtel Limited, *Regional Considerations: Strait of Canso, Nova Scotia* (October 1967), A-1.

12 - Town of Port Hawkesbury, *Financial Problems of the Town of Port Hawkesbury;* Submission to the Department of Municipal Affairs, February 26, 1974 (mimeo.), pp. 1-2.

13 - Graham, Napier, Hébert and Associates Ltd., *Project 3.9: Junior-Senior High School and Associated Community Facilities, Port Hawkesbury, Nova Scotia, Report II,* Vol. I: *Complete Project Information,* p. 212.

14 - *Ibid.,* pp. 263-264. The Principal of Centennial Elementary School reported a population fluctuation of 700; 605; 682; within a period of months.

15 - *County Profile: Richmond,* p. 37.

16 - *County Profile: Inverness*, p. 36.

17 - *County Profile: Richmond*, p. 37.

18 - *Ibid.*

19 - Graham, Napier, *et al., op. cit.*, p. 209.

20 - *County Profile: Inverness*, p. 36.

21 - *County Profile: Richmond*, p. 37.

22 - Graham, Napier, *et al., op. cit.*, p. 187.

23 - *Ibid.*, p. 255.

24 - *Ibid.*, p. 256.

25 - *Ibid., passim.*

26 - *Ibid.*, p. 277.

27 - *Ibid.*, s. 4, *passim.*

28 - *Financial Problems of the Town of Port Hawkesbury*, Appendix 2.

29 - *Ibid.*, Appendix 1.

30 - *County Profile: Inverness*, p. 38. The main cause of high rents, however, was the demand for accomodation during the construction boom.

31 - Graham, Napier, *et al., op. cit.*, p. 267.

32 - *Ibid.*

33 - Canadian Bechtel Ltd., *op. cit.*

34 - Graham, Napier, *et al., op. cit.*, pp. 281-282. See also pp. 256, 276 and 333.

35 - See *ibid.*, pp. 204, 208, 237, 269, 282, and 295.

36 - See *ibid.*, pp. 217, 215, 281, and 282.

37 - *Ibid.,* pp. 256-257.

38 - *Ibid.,* p. 256. See also p. 282.

39 - Nova Scotia Department of Municipal Affairs, Community Planning Division, *Proposed Port Hawkesbury Development Plan* (Halifax: May 1968), p. 44.

40 - *Industrial Development Conference.*

41 - *Proposed Port Hawkesbury Development Plan,* p. 1.

42 - Interview with Arthur J. Langley, Jr., June 26, 1974. See also "Regional Development: Strait of Canso Area", *op. cit.,* p. 16; and various consultants' studies including J. Philip Vaughan, *Report to the Town of Port Hawkesbury on a Water and Sewer System,* August 1960; *Hawkesbury Project, Inverness-Richmond Counties* (N.S. Department of Mines, March 1961); *Report on Municipal Water Supply and other Urgent Requirements of the Town of Port Hawkesbury* (Town of Port Hawkesbury Planning Commission, February 1967).

43 - Interview with Arthur J. Langley, Jr. Mr. Langley's view is shared by the other local officials questioned on this point.

44 - A reference to Premier Regan's view that the CGE plant was ill-placed is contained in an article by Rev. Andy Hogan in *The 4th Estate,* April 26, 1973.

45 - "Regional Development: Strait of Canso Area", p. 10.

46 - *Industrial Development Conference,* p. 19.

47 - Canada, House of Commons, *Debates,* October 13, 1967, p. 3641.

48 - See MacNamara Engineering Limited, *An Industrial Park Plan: Point Tupper* (May 1968).

49 - Halifax *Chronicle-Herald,* October 19, 1968.

50 - Economic Consultants Limited, *op. cit.*

51 - *Ibid.,* pp. ii-iii.

52 - *Ibid.,* p. iii.

53 - *Industrial Development Conference,* p. 8.

54 - See Chapter 308, *Revised Statutes of Nova Scotia,* 1967; and Chapter 16, *Statutes of Nova Scotia,* 1969.

55 - See R.S. Lang, *Nova Scotia Municipal and Regional Planning in the Seventies: Report / Evaluation of the Town Planning Act Review* (Halifax: Nova Scotia Department of Municipal Affairs and Central Mortgage and Housing Corp., 1972.)

56 - *Ibid.,* p. 15.

57 - Hans Foerstel, "Regional Planning in Nova Scotia: Approach, Process, Plan", *Proceedings: Nova Scotia Community Planning Conference,* November 6-7, 1969 (Halifax: Institute of Public Affairs, 1969), pp. 1-9, p. 1. See also Lang, *op. cit.,* pp. 176-186.

58 - Canadian Bechtel Limited, *op. cit.,*pp. 6-7.

59 - *Financial Problems of the Town of Port Hawkesbury.*

60 - Summarized in Community Planning Division's *Working Report VI* (Halifax: Department of Municipal Affairs, Community Planning Division, July 1968).

61 - *Proposed Port Hawkesbury Development Plan* (1968) pp. 1, 4 and 5.

62 - *Ibid.,* p. 31.

63 - *Ibid.,* pp. 39-40.

64 - Interview with Walter Fougere, Warden, Richmond County, June 26, 1974.

65 - *Strait of Canso Local Government Review: Steering Committee Report* (May 31, 1971), p. 1.

66 - *Ibid.,* p. 1.

67 - *Ibid.* See also T.J. Plunkett Associates, Ltd., *A report Outlining Proposals for Municipal Consolidation in the*

Strait of Canso Local Government Review Area, (Montreal: March 10, 1971).

68 - Interview with Alex Harris, Strait Area Development Co-ordinator, June 25, 1974.

69 - Nova Scotia Royal Commission on Education, Public Services and Provincial Municipal Relations, *Report (Graham Report)* (Halifax: 1974), II. 5-297-300.

70 - See Canada Department of Regional Economic Expansion, *Annual Reports,* for the period.

71 - See Graham, Napier, *et al., op.cit., passim.* Comments on the effects of Project 3.9 are derived from various interviews conducted in Port Hawkesbury, particularly those with Mayor W.J. MacLean, Alex Harris, Rev. David Price and Don Beaton, who was responsible for administering certain aspects of the project.

72 - Interview with Hector Hortie, Regional Director General, Department of Regional Economic Expansion, June, 1975.

73 - *Canada-Nova Scotia Subsidiary Agreement, Strait of Canso Area Development, 1975,* pp. 1-2.

74 - *Terms of Reference for Port Hastings-Port Hawkesbury-Point Tupper Development Plan* (draft, April 22, 1974, mimeo.).

75 - *Financial Problems of the Town of Port Hawkesbury,* p. 5.

76 - *Graham Report,* II. 5 - 286.

77 - *Financial Problems of the Town of Port Hawkesbury,* p. 9.

78 - *Ibid.,* p. 2.

79 - *Ibid.,* p. 3.

80 - See *Industrial Development Conference.* One local journalist estimated that, in 1973, only 15 per cent of the employees at the Gulf Refinery were originally Strait residents. *The 4th Estate,* "Ecology '73", October 1973.

81 - Various interviews.

82 - Steering Committee *Report, op.cit.,* p. 2.

83 - David Bentley, *Chronicle-Herald,* February 1, 1973.

84 - Interview with Mayor W.J. MacLean, June 27, 1974. Another issue in which local rivalries are currently delaying agreement is the proposal that a Port Commission be set up for the Strait of Canso.

85 - Confidential source.

IV. The Provincial Approach to Development

1 - John F. Graham, *Fiscal Adjustment and Economic Development* (Toronto: University of Toronto Press, 1963), p. 46.

2 - Canadian Tax Foundation, *The National Finances, 1970 - 71* (Toronto, 1970), p. 144.

3 - R.W. Phidd, "Regional Development Policy", in G. Bruce Doern and V. Seymour Wilson (eds.), *Issues in Canadian Public Policy* (Toronto: MacMillan, 1974), pp. 166-203, at pp. 185 and 186.

4 - See T.N. Brewis, *Regional Economic Policies in Canada* (Toronto: MacMillan, 1969), especially chs. 10 and 12.

5 - See W. MacKinnon, *The Policies of Development: The P.E.I. Development Plan* (unpublished M.A. thesis, Dalhousie University, 1972).

6 - See, for example, the emphasis on regional planning in the 1969 / 1970 *Annual Report* of DREE.

7 - See Phidd, *op. cit.; Atlantic Provinces Economic Council, Fifth Annual Review: The Atlantic Economy* (Halifax: 1971); and Douglas M. Johnston *et al., Coastal Zone: Framework for Management in Atlantic Canada* (Halifax: Institute of Public Affairs Dalhousie University, 1975), pp. 70-72.

8 - Brewis, *op.cit.,* p. 204. The tension between the planning and industrial incentives programs of DREE and its pre-

decessors is discussed in Carole MacKaay, *Canadian Regionalism: The Atlantic Development Board: A Case Study* (unpublished M.A. thesis, McGill University, 1969).

9 - DREE,*Annual Report,* 1972-1973, p. 3.

10 - See DREE, *Annual Reports,* 1970-71 to 1972-73.

11 - Phidd, *op.cit.,* p. 171.

12 - *Ibid.*

13 - Roy E. George, *The Life and Times of Industrial Estates Limited* (Halifax: Institute of Public Affairs, Dalhousie University, 1974), p. 32.

14 - See the *Lunenburg Progress-Enterprise,* most issues, November 1974-February 1975.

15 - *Graham Report,* II. 2-17.

16 - *Ibid.,* p. 17.

17 - J.M. Beck, *The Government of Nova Scotia* (Toronto: University of Toronto Press, 1957), pp. 208ff.

18 - *Ibid.,* p. 208.

19 - See Industrial Estates Act, *RSNS,* 1967, c. 139.

20 - George, *op. cit.,* p. 6.

21 - Memorandum of Agreement, 25 September 1957, between the Province and Industrial Estates Limited, Part VI, s. 6.

22 - *Ibid.,* Part IV, s. 1.

23 - See George, *op. cit.,* ch. 7.

24 - Michael Bradfield, *Provincial Development Corporations* (Halifax: Atlantic Provinces Economic Council, Seventh Annual Review, 1973), p. 45.

25 - See George, *op. cit.,* pp. 20-21.

26 - *Ibid.,* pp. 41-42.

27 - *Ibid.*

28 - *Ibid.*, pp. 53-54.

29 - Interview, July 10, 1974.

30 - *RSNS* 1967, c. 138.

31 - See Voluntary Planning Act, *RSNS* 1967, c. 332.

32 - *Ibid.*, s. 3.

33 - *Ibid.*, s. 4.

34 - *First Plan: For Economic Development to 1968*)Halifax: Nova Scotia Voluntary Planning Board, February, 1966).

35 - Geoffrey Stevens, *Stanfield*, p. 32.

36 - Special Committee, *Report of 27 October 1970* (mimeo.), p. 3.

37 - *Report of 27 October 1970*, p. 4.

38 - Public Service Act, *SNS,* 1970-71, c. 56, ss. 7-9.

39 - *Ibid.*, s. 8 (a).

40 - *Ibid.*, s. 8 (b).

41 - Interview with D. MacDonald, Secretary, Voluntary Planning Board, Jan. 1974.

42 - *Graham Report,* II. 18-17.

43 - George, *op. cit.*, pp. 53-54.

44 - A.P. Pross, *The Statutory Basis of Provincial and Municipal Planning in Nova Scotia: A Review* (Halifax: Institute of Public Affairs, Dalhousie University, 1974).

45 - See George, *op. cit.*, and *Graham Report.*

46 - Pross, *op. cit.*

47 - *Graham Report,* II. 2-81.

48 - Beck, *op. cit.,* p. 214.

49 - See Lang, *op. cit.,* p. 15.

50 - *Ibid.*

51 - *Ibid.;* also *Graham Report;* and Pross, *op. cit.*

52 - See Pross, *op. cit.*

53 - Lang, *op. cit.,* pp. 176-186.

54 - *Graham Report,* II. 18-36 and II. 6-278.

55 - Nova Scotia, Order-in-Council 69-517, May 29, 1969.

56 - Halifax *Chronicle-Herald,* February 11, 1970.

57 - Halifax *Chronicle-Herald,* February 1, 1971; and *Financial Post,* January 2, 1971. A fairly extensive account of the Secretariat's brief history is found in R.S. Lang, *Nova Scotia Municipal and Regional Planning in the Seventies: Report / Evaluation of the Town Planning Act Review* (Halifax: Nova Scotia Department of Municipal Affairs and Central Mortgage and Housing Corporation, 1972), ch. 5.

58 - Halifax *Chronicle-Herald,* January 6, 1971.

59 - *The 4th Estate,* Halifax, April 6, 1972. A year later Joseph Zatzman, Chairman of the Nova Scotia Resources Development Board, told a Dalhousie University regional development conference that "the policy of development that we have [in Nova Scotia] is that there is no policy. That is our policy." *Chronicle-Herald,* May 12, 1973. See also, briefs presented to the Graham Commission by Voluntary Planning, the Nova Scotia Federation of Agriculture, and Mayor Sherman Zwicker of Lunenburg, *Chronicle-Herald,* November 17, 1971 and January 13, 1972.

60 - See Marion R. Haviland, "The Nova Scotia Cabinet: Organization and Changing Needs", March 1973 (mimeo.).

61 - *Ibid.,* pp. 13-14.

62 - *Graham Report,* II. 18-18.

V. Broadening the Scope of Development Planning

1 - *Proposed Port Hawkesbury Development Plan,* Nova Scotia Department of Municipal Affairs, Community Planning Division, 1968, p. 1.

2 - Confidential interview.

3 - Confidential interview.